Embodiment and Legal Theory

This book addresses the importance of the body in legal theory, through an analysis of the film *Fifty Shades of Grey*.

As physical beings, we experience law in sensations of outrage when it is applied unethically, righteousness when it finds justice, and joy when it establishes partnerships in marriage. Our bodies feel and know law. In *Embodiment and Legal Theory*, it is argued that our bodies also theorise law. It is proposed that our bodies are involved in comprehending, negotiating, and reimagining the legal concepts that shape our lives. As a medium designed to engage us by stimulating our bodily reactions of tears, laughter, shock, and titillation, cinema provides an ideal site for exploring how bodies participate in legal arguments and the construction of legal meaning. For this reason, through a deep analysis of the film *Fifty Shades of Grey* (2015), this book presents a theory of embodied jurisprudence.

At the intersection of legal theory and film studies, this book will appeal to students and scholars in both these areas, as well as in criminology and cultural studies.

Kirsty Duncanson is Senior Lecturer in Crime, Justice and Legal Studies in the Department of Social Inquiry at La Trobe University, Melbourne.

Embodiment and Legal Theory

Law in Fifty Shades of Grey

Kirsty Duncanson

Routledge
Taylor & Francis Group
a GlassHouse Book

First published 2025
by Routledge
4 Park Square, Milton Park, Abingdon, Oxon OX14 4RN

and by Routledge
605 Third Avenue, New York, NY 10158

Routledge is an imprint of the Taylor & Francis Group, an informa business

A GlassHouse book

British Library Cataloguing-in-Publication Data
A catalogue record for this book is available from the British Library

Library of Congress Cataloging-in-Publication Data
Names: Duncanson, Kirsty, author.
Title: Embodiment and legal theory : law in Fifty Shades of Grey / Kirsty Duncanson.
Description: Abingdon, Oxon [UK] ; New York, NY : Routledge, 2025. | Includes bibliographical references and index.
Identifiers: LCCN 2024036982 (print) | LCCN 2024036983 (ebook) | ISBN 9780367335069 (hardback) | ISBN 9781032951270 (paperback) | ISBN 9780429330414 (ebook)
Subjects: LCSH: Law in motion pictures. | James, E. L. Fifty shades trilogy. | Law—Philosophy. | Law in literature. | Sex customs in literature.
Classification: LCC K3786 .D86 2025 (print) | LCC K3786 (ebook) | DDC 340/.1—dc23/eng/20240813
LC record available at https://lccn.loc.gov/2024036982
LC ebook record available at https://lccn.loc.gov/2024036983

ISBN: 978-0-367-33506-9 (hbk)
ISBN: 978-1-032-95127-0 (pbk)
ISBN: 978-0-429-33041-4 (ebk)

DOI: 10.4324/9780429330414

Typeset in Times New Roman
by Apex CoVantage, LLC

Contents

Acknowledgements

First and foremost, thank you, Helen Forster. Treasured friend for the longest time. This book began in our conversations and evolved through the paper we wrote together. Life got in the way of building it into a collaborative project. Our conversations are always full of cynicism and rage, critique, and despair. I love you endlessly and am lucky to have you in my life. I wish we got to see each other more.

This book has taken an eternity to write, its authorship has involved recovery from cancer, solo parenting – solo parenting through the most intense COVID lockdowns, university restructures, and so on.

I could not have kept writing without the endless support of Su Robjohn – Mama and Nana extraordinaire.

Laura Griffin and Maria Elander, thank you both for your feedback on the draft that challenged me and took me deeper. It is an incredible honour for me that two such powerful and thoughtful scholars dedicated their precious time to making my work better.

My message group coven, Laura Griffin, Hannah Robert, and Katie Weise kept me sane with memes, pizza nights, and actual significant and lifesaving acknowledgement, support, and advice. Thank you for listening to my audio messages. Thank you Emma Henderson for our weekly research and rage meetings. Thank you Advanced Jazz crew and Body Electric for the sequins. Thank you Georgia Phelan and Matt Mitchell for the book chats.

Elke Sundblom: the memory cake, the phenomenal fake snow disaster of 2021, the impetuousness, and the incisive questions. Sandy Sundblom: the stories and inventions, the great tooth-extracting incident of 2017, the dedication to social justice and the ceaseless leaping. I love you both more than you will ever know.

Prelude

> A woman steps out of an elevator, removing a trench coat to display a narrow, plum dress. It is not quite tight and not quite revealing. The neckline and tapered waist hint towards exposure but remain professionally concealing. The cap sleeves gesture towards shoulder pads and power-suits. The woman holds a document file. This is an empowered woman, transformed from the floral-shirted, pony-tailed girl who tripped into the hero's office at the beginning of the film. Shot from the hero's point of view, the heroine returns the gaze, holding eye contact: resisting the power exercised by the masculine evaluation of women's bodies. Her resistance is emphasised by her removal of his hand from her back as they walk towards the boardroom. "Business meeting" she utters firmly.

Anticipation permeates this brief clip. Marking one point in the emotional undulation of the film's erotic romance, the clip encourages the audience to hope for sexual play in the scene that will follow. While the modest but alluring dress contributes to the anticipation, it also signifies female empowerment. The *frisson* of this dual promise is more overtly denoted by the document file. The file is a contract: a tool for negotiating the structure and boundaries of the couple's relationship, and more specifically the submissive role to which the heroine has been asked to consent in lieu of a traditional romance. The contract promises Ana the power to discuss the terms of the proposed role as an equal with her male lover. It also lists a range of sex acts and toys. In its joint promise of sexual activity and gender equality, the contract echoes contemporary promises of sexual assault legislation that situates consent as the condition of legitimate sex. For the film's audience, the document file is potentially both empowering and titillating. The sequence physically reverberates with a sexualised discourse of contemporary sexual assault law.

Focusing on the sensual experience of cinema and law, this book argues that bodies are involved in the theorising of legal ideas; that they practice embodied jurisprudence. This is to understand that bodies make and recreate the meaning of legal concepts like contract and consent through the practice of their daily lives.

DOI: 10.4324/9780429330414-1

Introduction

As physical beings we experience law in sensations – outrage when it is applied unfairly; righteous satisfaction when it overcomes injustice; joy when it recognises the unity of couples in marriage. Our bodies feel and know law. This book argues that we also use our bodies to *theorise* law. That is, our bodies are involved in comprehending, negotiating, and reimagining the legal concepts that shape our lives. Cinema is a medium deliberately designed to engage us by stimulating our bodies to react with tears, shock, apprehension, laughter, and titillation. It is also woven through with stories and assumptions about law. As such, cinema provides an ideal site for exploring how bodies participate in legal arguments and the construction of legal meaning. Through an analysis of a single scene within the film *Fifty Shades of Grey* (Taylor-Johnson 2015), *Embodiment and Legal Theory* presents a theory of embodied jurisprudence.

The overarching contention is that bodies practice legal philosophy. Bodies grapple with legal ideas and generate legal meaning. To make this argument, I examine one Scene (*the Scene*) from three points of entry with a focus on a set of legal concepts at the film's heart. *The Scene* is a mock business meeting in which the central couple negotiate the structure of their intimacy using a contract. This cinematic contract echoes the contractual nature of contemporary rape law and its preoccupation with consent. In the *First and Second Readings* (*The Frisson of Sexual Agency* and *The Discomforts of Subordination*), I analyse *the Scene* through the lens of two ostensibly antithetical feminist legal critiques. From an optimistic liberal feminist perspective, *the Scene* can be read as empowering for women through its contract. Such a reading is supported by further cinematic elements connoting liberal values. Concurrently, *the Scene* can be read as disempowering using poststructuralist feminism to reveal patterns of gendered subordination throughout liberal philosophy, particularly in the context of contract and consent. These are only two of many potential feminist legal interpretations. They can be entertained by the one feminist (me) simultaneously, and they may not be shared in the same way by other liberal or poststructuralist feminists. By presenting two oppositional feminist legal readings I demonstrate the presence of legal ideas

DOI: 10.4324/9780429330414-2

within *the Scene*, while also illustrating that those ideas can be read in various and contradictory ways. Further than this, I use the availability of multiple readings as evidence of the interpretive labour exercised by consumers as they process cinematic code and grapple with cultural references: filtering images and narratives through pre-existing logic frameworks; embracing new ideas while ignoring or rejecting others; and actively making sense of the film. I establish the agency of consumers, particularly consumers of "women's fiction," in the chapter *Reader Agency*. Because the film relies on legal concepts to tell its story, the active interpretation of consumers is also a negotiation of legal concepts. In this way, audiences are engaged in theorising legal meaning, or jurisprudence.

My *Third Reading* (*Legal Sensations* and *Doing Jurisprudence*) attends to the physicality with which cinematic interpretation is performed. As an erotic (pornographic) romance, *Fifty Shades* stirs the bodies of its audience to arousal. This has implications for how bodies interact with the text. I am also interested in the role of sound in the meaningful enjoyment of *the Scene*, which encourages consumers to *lose themselves* – suspend their disbelief – in the text and identify deeply with its characters and ideas. The concepts of contract and consent are tangled through these stimulating cinematic effects. But I go further to map the phenomenological labour consumers exert to prepare themselves for *loss of self* and achieve *jouissance* at the cinema; to identify with the intensities of the feeling of multiple characters and the ideas available in the text. Part of consumer pleasure is embodied dissonance through loving and criticising what is consumed through active embodied analysis, discussion with others and the creation of secondary texts. In the case of *Fifty Shades* the secondary texts include reflective discussions of intimacy and doing sex differently. Consumers experiment with different ways of understanding sex, sexuality, and gender while they watch, and after, in discussions with friends and strangers, in their creation of secondary texts, and in the practice of their own gender, sex, and sexuality. I argue that the sensual experience and practice of consuming the film are also active sensual engagement with legal ideas. Through these encounters, agentic consumers use their embodied knowledge from outside the cinema to interpret *the Scene*. They also use what they garner from within *the Scene* to help make sense of the world beyond the cinema. In this manner, audiences are practising embodied philosophy. Further than this, due to the legal content of the scene, audiences are performing embodied philosophies of law.

Ultimately, I am arguing that a philosophical consideration of law, as contract and consent, is performed by bodies at the cinema while enjoying (and abhorring) *Fifty Shades*. I call this active engagement *embodied jurisprudence*.

Before I attend to the body of my argument, let me set out the theory and scholarship informing my work and my interdisciplinary analytical practice. I begin with legal theory and follow with a brief explanation of relevant sexual assault scholarship, a methodology for my cinematic analysis, theories concerning embodied philosophy and an explanation of the why and what of *Fifty Shades*.

Legal Theory

Much knowledge about what law is, how it works, and what it means is garnered from popular culture by those who (like myself) did not attend law school. But also by those who did (Sharp 2016). Cultural legal scholars are fascinated by the relationship between law and legal knowledge, television, film, books, music, comics, and art (see Leiboff and Sharp 2016; Crawley 2016; Tranter 2012; Duncanson 2020; Elander 2014; Giddens 2015). Initially, studies of law and film concentrated on the accuracy of cinematic representations of law. They argued that popular culture reflects commonly shared understandings (and misunderstandings) and revealed cultural assumptions about gendered and raced legal practice (Salzman and Dunwoody 2005; Podlas 2008; Greenfield et al. 2010; Sherwin 2000). This work continues to provide important insights into the pervasive quality of legal ideas across non-legal texts. Increasingly, however, cultural legal studies argue that pop culture texts are neither strictly right nor wrong, neither even inaccurate nor correct in their representations of law. Rather, through their in/accuracy these texts *produce legal meaning*. Further still, cultural legal studies demonstrate that *consumers of popular culture actively produce legal knowledge in concert with these texts* (MacNeil 2007).

Cultural legal studies understand popular culture as "a domain where law is practiced, negotiated, legitimised and embodied" (Collis and Bainbridge 2005, 162). Its texts are sources of law (Manderson 2003). But more than this, its texts are conduits through which legal concepts are evaluated, reiterated, critiqued, disputed, transformed, and recreated (Moran et al. 2004). They are sites in which law is theorised by "ordinary" folk. MacNeil (2007) calls this *lex populi* or "popular jurisprudence."

My argument is that popular jurisprudence is embodied – practised through the whole body of each lay legal theorist while consuming texts of popular culture. To understand the body's role in popular jurisprudence I rely on a wealth of feminist-informed scholarship that reveals deep entanglements between law and bodies. Cover (1986, 1601) states that "legal interpretation takes place in a field of pain and death," arguing that punitive sentences restrict bodily movement and the intimate touch between close friends and relatives through imprisonment. The same legal interpretation can also remove life. Other legal theorists show more subtle ways in which bodies are regulated by law. For example, movement, appearance, and experience are policed by the crimino-legal gaze: law stipulates when, where and how bodies might be naked, engaged in sex (Grabham 2009), fighting (Hanna 2000–2001), or creating art (Young 2005). It dictates when a body can or cannot consent to injury or wounding, tattoos and piercing (Green 2001), circumcision or other modification (Rogers 2003). In these instances, law shapes bodies, behaviour, and the procedures bodies can undergo.

Law categorises and determines bodies as sexed, raced, and politically in/capable, amongst so many other things. For example, Lord Justice Ormrod set out a four-point test to legally determine a person's sex (Corbett v Corbett [otherwise Ashley] [1970], 83). In doing so, his judgment also established definitions for sexual intercourse and marriage. These definitions were applied for the purposes of sex-sensitive laws, but most specifically those concerning marriage. The UK *Gender Recognition Act 2004* has since enabled people to apply to receive certification to change their sexed legal status but with a choice between binary categories. More recently, the High Court of Australia ruled that the NSW Registry of Births, Deaths, and Marriages could record a person's sex as "not specific" ((2014) 250 CLR 490 *NSW Registrar* v *Norrie*). Marriage equality across the common law world has almost enabled us to take for granted that people of the same sex may marry (within a monogamous norm); sexual offence reform and repealed sodomy laws have begun to broaden legal understandings of sex. Sex and the configurations of sexual intimacy are delimited by law.

Identification and categorization of bodies as raced, sexed, classed, and abled has characterized immigration, citizenship, and suffrage law (Clark 1996; Bloodsworth-Lugo and Lugo-Lugo 2010). Following the arguments of Foucault, legal theorists demonstrate how such practices produce the very bodies they appear to regulate. Possibilities for bodily form and identity are opened and shut down by legal technologies and decision-making processes. In this manner, bodies come to be known and to know themselves through the law's eyes.

Correspondingly, legal scholarship has revealed the demands law makes on bodies. MacNeil (1998) shows how rights discourse requires bodies to conform with the hidden bodies of law's authors and retainers. Rogers (2003) demonstrates the way law silences non-conforming bodies. Disability may be recognised, so long as it is presented to meet specific bodily configurations (Campbell 1999). Gay rights can be granted, within the parameters of appropriately expressed same-sex desire (Morgan 1993–1994; Baird 2006). Kamler and MacLean (1997) and Manderson and Turner (2006) reveal ways in which law schools don't simply teach students law, but also train students to move their bodies according to implicit rules, and "like a lawyer." By fulfilling these demands, bodies exercise law and legal meaning as they mimic legally preferred performances.

Getting deeper into material form, some legal theorists argue that law works through bodies as emotions, desires, and sensations. We might understand these in terms of affect. "Affect" names intensities of feelings and resonances that pass through and between bodies, even when those bodies are not human (as in the relationship between consumer and screen). Affects are "forces . . . impulses and energies" that move or drive us (Iedema 2021, 18).

They are theorised as pre-discursive, before language: immediate, unmediated, and unrepresented (18). They are "visceral forces beneath, alongside or generally *other than* conscious knowing" (Gregg and Seigworth 2010, 1); the "chasm between" discourse and feeling or emotion (Iedema 2021, v). They can be recognised in the "not yet of never-quite-knowing" (Gregg and Seigworth 2010, 9). These are sensations that seem to not quite signify or convey meaning, as they sweep, flutter, course through or unsettle our bodies. Sometimes affects are momentary and sometimes they stick, linger, or haunt (Gregg and Seigworth 2010, 1). Situated so much in the body, affects can seem prior to culture (natural) and before intellectual processing. As such, they can appear to defy representational analysis. Yet they are increasingly a site of both cinematic and socio-legal interrogation.

Philippopoulos-Mihalopoulos (2013) exposes the omnipresence of law's interference with seemingly every intensity of feeling. Law "guides bodies into corridors of sensory compulsion," thus allowing "certain sensory options to come forth while suppressing others" (35). Theorising *atmospheres* of law, he (35) demonstrates that law lets us "eat in a certain way, smell, touch people in a certain way (and not other)." Law does this because "every surface, smell, colour, taste is regulated by some form of law . . . intellectual property, planning . . . environmental law, health and safety regulations, and so on" (35). Similarly, Howes (2019, 175 original emphasis) asserts that law is a "*sense-making activity*," while Hamilton et al. (2016, 2) observe that "legal techniques seek to control and discipline the human experience of the senses." Law shapes our sensorial experiences through its pervasive regulation of objects, actions, processes, ownership, and plans.

Experiences of unfairness or violations of justice "trigger a heightened sense of taste and smell" (Skarlicki et al. 2013, 852). Justice is "something felt deeply" (Johnson 2009, 817). Gunby and Carline (2020) investigate the affects barristers experience when working sexual assault trials. With Murray, they (Carline et al. 2021) consider barristers' strategic use of affects at trial to influence jury decision-making. Leiboff (2015, 80) argues that we respond to law as an "embodied mind" and "without being consciously aware of it." Our bodily responses inform our understanding of justice and law. Relatedly, Grabham (2009, 345–346) observes that "emotions permeate legal regulation," arguing that touch creates new legal knowledge to shape and infiltrate "law's various governing and knowledge-forming processes." We feel, see, smell, and taste justice and law; we respond through our emotional, sensorial bodies. Law is woven through our affective experience and affective experience influences the shape and meaning of law.

Through each encounter with law, bodies build legal knowledge, not only intellectually but also somatically (Manderson and Turner 2006). Bodies *feel* law's meaning in every judgment, categorisation, limitation, and freedom. They experience intensities of feelings, sensations, and affects that appear to resist signification but are felt meaningfully in the body. As such, bodies experience legal interpretation as they move, touch, rest, eat, and dream. Bodies interpret, perform, adjust, and make material law. Thus, we each carry knowledge of the law in our bodies as much as we hold it in our consciousness. Maybe more so. Consequently, as we move through our daily rituals, brushing up against all those objects and through those atmospheres resonating with legal significance, our bodily legal knowledge interacts with other manifestations of legal interpretation. Our bodies are constantly negotiating legal concepts and interpreting law. Our bodies practice jurisprudence.

Rape Law

Sexual assault is a particularly bodily field of law. Establishing a range of criminal offences, sexual assault laws inform some of the most physically intimate moments of our lives: bodies touching or being touched; penetrating or being penetrated; body parts exposed; specific and specifically signifying acts; and the locations in which they all might be conducted. The structure of sexual offences in most common law jurisdictions now places consent as a transformative core, distinguishing many lawful from unlawful acts, while itemising conditions of personhood (age, unconsciousness, "mental capacity," intoxication) that vitiate or invalidate consent (Munro 2008, 924). Consent is "the focal point of sexual assault" (Cowan 2007, 92). By prioritising consent, the legal ideal of sex becomes contractual, involving exchanges comprising proposals of, and consent to, a range of activities.

The centrality of consent to sexual assault, and the contractual structure of rape, in particular, is a critical point of feminist jurisprudential divergence. Liberal feminists have argued that contractual conversations about sex have the potential to empower women to better navigate intimacy. Additionally, liberal feminist law reform has enabled recognition of non-heteronormative sexual violence, such that in some jurisdictions persons do not require a vagina to be a victim, nor does a perpetrator require a penis. Meanwhile, post-structuralist feminists trouble the extent of empowerment available through a liberal framework, interrogating the gendered narratives and assumptions persistently shaping contract theory.

But sexual *violence* is more than questions of consent and contract. It is harm of a sexual nature including, but not limited to, that defined by law as rape or sexual assault. Critical race scholars demonstrate that for women of colour sexual violence is "frequently the product of intersecting patterns of racism and sexism" (Crenshaw 1994, 94). Sexual violence is a tool of colonisation, exploitation, and white supremacy: "a form of control and domination" (Ryan 2020, 121). Focusing on the experience of women with developmental disabilities, Razack (1994, 893) interrogates the ways in which "women are positioned in law differently and unequally in relation to each other." She argues that if feminists do not attend to these differences, we are complicit in maintaining law's taxonomies (categories) and marginalisation practices. Queer theory digs "deeper into the dominant narratives around sexual violence," including those that persist in the feminist poststructuralist deconstruction of sexual assault law (Patterson 2016). *Queering* sexual assault works to expose heteronormative myths that sexual violence is perpetrated by cis-gendered men against cis-gendered women (Ison 2020, 153). Building evidence demonstrates that lesbian, gay, bisexual, trans*, non-binary, and queer people experience sexual violence at equivalent, if not higher rates, than straight cis-women, and that this violence is often related to heterosexism (153). Debates and challenges keep feminism mutating and multiplying while revealing different ways in which we can understand and address sexual violence as part of further structures of violence throughout society (Patterson 2016).

In this book, I focus on liberal and poststructuralist feminist jurisprudence as a potent, antagonistic dyad so I can interrogate how jurisprudence is embodied. They present interconnected examples of legal interpretation – related but quarrelsome. Additionally, their shared focus on consent and contract in rape law makes their philosophical logic exceptionally accessible when reading for cinematic legal theory. Thus, while *the Scene* can be read through a liberal feminist lens as celebrating gender equality through autonomy and neutrality, a poststructuralist critique reveals persistent paradoxes concerning sex, neutrality, autonomy, and agency that hinder the realisation of such equality. In their antagonism, the two feminist philosophies provide material to demonstrate coexisting legal interpretations within the consumption of a single film scene.

Both liberal and poststructuralist feminist philosophies have made important contributions to theorising law and sex. However, neither has been adequate to the task of comprehensively addressing sexual violence as a non-homogenic phenomena. Both have excluded and silenced victims/survivors while missing cohorts of perpetrators. However, neither field of feminist scholarship is static nor homogenous. Moreover, similarly ideologically aligned feminists might easily disagree with either or both of my feminist interpretations of *the Scene*. Theory is dynamic and always in development. Additionally, many feminists subscribe to liberal and poststructuralist theory simultaneously, critically, and strategically in potential contradiction, but also while engaging with further legal theory and methodologies. Jurisprudence is never pure but entangled with its cultural heritage, gaining strength from alliances. It is dissonant throughout its inconsistencies and assumptions.

My purpose in my first two readings is to reveal that both liberal and poststructuralist readings of consent and contract are available in *the Scene*. An individual consumer might engage in both simultaneously, while also agreeing and disagreeing with *my* feminist informed interpretations. This all provides evidence that consumers are negotiating varying legal ideas and that this is jurisprudence. In my third reading of *the Scene*, I implement embodied cinema analysis to demonstrate how jurisprudence is practised by the film's audience bodies.

Cinema Theory

Cinema is a particularly viscerally engaging medium, infamous in its earliest form for making people leap from their seats and run from the theatre (Gunning 1990). Cinema is also rich with stories, images, and ideas about law. As such, it is an ideal site for exploring how legal philosophy involves bodies. I, therefore, investigate *the Scene* from *Fifty Shades* by applying analytical methods derived from cinema studies to show how the bodies of its consumers practice jurisprudence. Cinema studies is a broad field. However, my methodology uses tools for investigating the generation of meaning in the interaction between text and consuming bodies. While the first two readings of *the Scene* rely on semiotic analysis, for the third reading I draw on theories of *signifiance*, *jouissance,* and *shimmers*, focusing on arousal and affects stimulated by sound and the film's pornographic conventions. I demonstrate how consumers are encouraged to "lose themselves" in *the Scene*, suspend their disbelief, identify, and merge with the text. Although losing yourself in the text might seem passive, consumers actively wrestle with cinematic stimuli to enjoy the sensation and make sense of *the Scene* with a contract at its centre. Thus, I argue that consumers are performing jurisprudence.

Predominantly, cinematic analysis is ocularcentric – preoccupied by images (Del Rio 2000). However, consuming cinema is sensual: involving tears, laughter, racing heartbeats, intake of breath, elation, and arousal. Williams (2008, 1) observes that while much

> has been written about the ways we lose ourselves or identify with those glorious, magnified images of human bodies in movement . . . much less has been written about the ways we reencounter our own bodies, and our sensuality, in that process.

I follow work from the edges of cinema studies to develop an analysis that recognises the whole of the body in cinematic consumption and interpretation.

MacDougall (2006, 3) asserts that at the cinema we "see with our bodies." Bodies are actively encouraged to luxuriate in sensations triggered by images, sound, narrative, and the context of the viewing space (Hanich 2018). At the same time, the cinematic text relies on and engages with, knowledge held by each body to communicate ideas, stories, and arguments during the limited time available in a discrete 90-minute text. Thus, cinematic meaning is generated through an interaction between text and bodies.

MacDougall (2006) describes embodied viewing as a kind of frustrated mimesis, in which bodies imagine themselves performing the action on screen or responding as if that action were unfolding within physical proximity. As though dreaming, viewing bodies may not actually perform the acts, but muscles remember the experience of each movement, and nerves remember touch. For Sobchack (2004) the experience is more reflexive. She (77) writes that while watching, "I will reflexively turn towards my own carnal and sensual being to touch myself touching, smell myself smelling, taste myself tasting, and in sum, feel my own sensuality." Audience bodies feel the caress without being caressed, taste fruit without taking anything into their mouths, feel the ache without doing the exercise. The pleasure of cinema involves a haunting within the flesh of remembered or imagined sensation.

Through these ghostly sensations, our bodies interpret the encoded text of cinema. Our bodies make sense of the sensual text because *both* the text *and* our bodily knowledge are created through shared discourses of sensational significance. According to Sobchack (63), meaning is produced at the cinema using our "entire bodily being" which is "informed by the full history and carnal knowledge of our acculturated sensorium." Through our lived experiences, our bodies have been trained to attach specific meaning and knowledge to an extensive range of sensations. Sobchack (76) calls this the "*subjectively felt lived body*." Films are designed to trigger sensations that are rich with meaning, in a manner that brings inestimable interpretative possibilities. Ott (2010) describes a similar body he calls the "*experienced body*." This body applies the knowledge of its experience from outside the specific cinema to its experience of watching what is presented within the specific cinema. Inside the cinema, it is an "*experiencing body*." The encounter of experienc<u>ed</u> and experienc<u>ing</u> body builds further experiential knowledge, recognising and reiterating shared assumptions, ideas, and stories, while undermining, transforming, and reworking others. Bodies leaving the cinema, thus have enhanced or reconfigured knowledges which might be used for subsequent cinema visits, but also (importantly) for life beyond.

Williams (2008) adds imaginary play to embodied cinematic knowledge. A body may not have experienced that which it feels while watching in order to engage with and create meaning through consuming film. Bodies might be encouraged to imagine experiencing new sensations. An illustrative example is the "kinky fuckery" represented in *Fifty Shades*. Growth in sex toy sales and online forum declarations of increased female libido have been read as evidence that the represented sex piqued women's interest and broadened their sexual horizons (Jones and Mills 2014). It could be theorised that *Fifty Shades* provoked the bodies of female consumers to imaginatively experience sexual practices which, hitherto, they had not explored, motivating them to purchase new toys and articulate their desire more explicitly.

Semiotics and *Shimmers*

To analyse embodied engagement with *the Scene*, my method is strongly informed by semiotics. I read *the Scene* by identifying and translating patterns of signs. Each sign is comprised of a *signifier* and its *signified*. The *signifier* is a written or spoken word, "sound pattern," image, object, or " 'material' element" (Saussure 2013, 76). The *signified* is a concept associated with the *signifier*. By breaking up language into these components, Saussure's work disrupts the assumed natural relationship between "a name and a thing," revealing instead that the meaning of a word is not inherent (Saussure 2013, 76). Rather, it is cultural and contextual. This uncoupling extends to all other material elements (signifiers) from which we derive meaning or significance. To recognise that the significance of a cinematic text involves the bodies of its audience, the material elements treated as signifiers include the intensities of feelings, sensations, and emotions we experience at the cinema.

In part, due to the discipline's debt to Saussurian semiotics, it can be difficult to explore manifold and dissonant interpretations using cinema analysis. Saussure asserted that the meaning of a signifier comes into being through its structural relationship with what it is not. Its meaning is determined in contradistinction from all other possible meanings ("dog" is not cat, is not bat, human, chair, etc). Meaning is thus generated through oppositional terms and "produced in conflict" (Steinbock 2019, 9). As the "choice of one term over another," signification is produced through binary structures: cat/dog, man/woman, thinking/feeling, seeing/touching (Barthes in Steinbock 2019, 9). As oppositional, each binary couplet suggests that the signs are mutually exclusive. Thus, if the signifier is identified as "man," "binary logic maintains that [the signifier] cannot be a woman" (D'Cruz 2020, 17). Further than this, "what does not fall neatly into either side of the binary unsettles presumed order and can acquire negative connotations for deviating from . . . the expectations of dominant culture" (17). Binaries strongly inform European logic, making it difficult to "think or communicate without oppositional logic" (17). A consequence of this paradigm, this model for understanding signification, is the academic interpretation of textual meaning as either one or another concept rather than both at once, liminal or flux – confounding distinctions (Steinbock 2019, 9). This fails to capture so many refractions of interpretative possibility.

Steinbock's (2019) trans* theorisation of *shimmers* enables the recognition of multiple simultaneous interpretations that may include apparent internal contradiction or dissonance. Their work helps to explore the activity of consumers navigating possible various meanings from one scene. Shimmers are material, but they are also metaphorical. They are the material that constitutes cinema, and they are the tiny meaningful signifiers consumers briefly grasp and process in order to understand the narratives offered to them.

Substantively, shimmers are the subdued play of light on tiny particles of dust, metal, glass, water, and even shiny plastic. Fireflies shimmer, as does bioluminescence in the waves at night. Shimmers continuously move and refract; they are elusive and ostensibly impossible to capture. They are "difficult to grasp as knowable entities" (Steinbock 2019, 8). Steinbock (8) analyses cinema as a manifestation of shimmers as a material play of light.

Shimmers are in the "flickering of frames with black spaces in between"; pixels; and machines that project patterns of shadow and luminous colour across darkened theatres.

Shimmers are also the tiniest and most fleeting of signifiers, potentially grasped and made to mean by consumers. Steinbock (2019, 10) draws on Barthes' association between shimmers and *nuance*. To be nuanced is to have subtle variation. Attention to nuance allows us to perceive minuscule gradations of difference like degrees of intensity in colour and shade (Barthes 2005). *Shimmers* as a metaphor for refracting signification counters the structural compulsion towards "the rational realm of well-focused categorisations and 'strong' ensuing differences" of semiotics (Moraru 2016, 292). Although *shimmers* can be elusive and difficult to grasp, attending to their flickering and to nuance – looking out for gradations of difference and multiple refracting significations – enables the perception of subtle degrees in variation that defy categorisation and the oppositional determination of signification. In this manner, *shimmers* inflect the semiotic method of this book.

Gregg and Seigworth (2010, 11) mark the bodily quality of *shimmers*. Appreciable refractions and gradients extend beyond what is visually discernible to include odour, space, speed, comportment, and reactions evoked in organ and tissue. In fact, Gregg and Steigworth (2010, 11) assert that affect theory is "at a level, an 'inventory of shimmers'" – a methodology for noticing microscopic fragments of emotion, affective moments, minuscule variances, and trajectories of intensity and sensation. The *shimmers* I attend to in my third reading of *the Scene* are embodied.

Although *shimmers* enable analysis of texts to recognise multiple interpretations, there are many conditions shaping individual consumers' ability to perceive the entire array available. At the same time, as an enhanced semiotics, comprehension of *shimmers* follows shared logic and cultures of signification. For starters, the capacity for a text *to shimmer* is enabled and restricted by means of production. Steinbock (2019, 8) refers to the tools used to measure and control light in cinematic production. For example, the "Shirley card" used to attune skin tone with light and colour processing used white skin as the standard, thereby privileging clarity and definition upon white actors over actors of colour. Some cinematic technologies and techniques dominate, establishing recognisable conventions. Others subvert them. Meantime, as "in-flux entities," the shimmering play of light is never completely governable (Steinbock 2019, 8). Refractions of light are influenced by the enculturated technologies that make them.

Correspondingly, consumer access to, and comprehension of, shimmers rely on training. Along the lines of Ott's (2010) experienc*ed* and experienc*ing* bodies, we each learn how to recognise various patterns of dark and light, and how to follow the directions of refracting twinkles. We then use our pre-existing frameworks of logic, "acculturated perceptual schema," and embodied philosophies to fix meaning onto what we grasp of the shimmers (Barthes in Steinbock

2019, 9). Steinbock (8) notes the compulsion to assimilate new information into established repertoires, calling this "the viewer's persistence of vision." Such compulsion persistently corrals interpretive compliance with dominant frameworks but cannot guarantee conformity. Our philosophical frameworks include those pertaining to law. For instance, rape trial jury research reveals that individual jurors will go to significant lengths to assimilate evidence into rape myth narratives (Ellison and Munro 2009). Further research suggests that if evidence cannot be assimilated, it is often ignored or forgotten (Duncanson and Henderson 2014). However, although most cinema consumers are literate in dominant logic frameworks, many are also familiar with divergent, subjugated, and counter-logics through shared communities of experienced divergence, marginalisation, and allegiance. Consumer capacity to grasp and take flight in all the directions of refracting shimmers depends on individual cultural histories, adherence to dominant philosophical frameworks, and openness to divergence, liminality, and dissonance.

Each viewer's persistence of vision can blind them to shimmers not relevant to themselves, even though those shimmers might be enjoyed by the person next to them at the cinema. Thus, while Steinbock (2019, 8) describes their own perception of wavering oscillations signifying with relevance to their trans* knowledge and experience, to non-trans* consumers the same shimmers might not be discernible, might be inscrutable, enigmatic, even seemingly deceptive, erroneous, or false. Perception and interpretation of shimmers "is subtly modified according to the angle of the subject's gaze," contingent on each consumer's history and training (Barthes 2005, 51). If we can imagine the refracting light perceived from different positions within a space, what we each see is a little unlike what everyone else is seeing. Thus, bodies in a cinema – each a differently acculturated sensorium – separately grasp refracting light particles and comprehend them otherwise from one another. This echoes Sobchack's (1992) assertion that cinematic meaning alters according to "'whose body' is watching." Similarly, Ahmed (2007, 125) observes that "what we may feel" of the *atmosphere* within a space, "depends on the angle of our arrival." The way we read a room, the way the room feels, and our affective response to it, is informed by the expectations, histories, and knowledge we bring with us, orienting the angle of our entrance into the space, informing the meaning produced by us about the space.

Although shimmers offer a potentially inexhaustible variety of readings of a single scene within a film, no single consumer can access them all. While we are generally compelled to comprehend dominant semiotics, most of us perceive the trajectories of refracted light that speak our unique blend of privilege and marginalisation. Blindness to so many light particles regularly relates to privilege. A key characteristic of privilege is not needing to learn the logic or conventions of those who are different from oneself. However, despite cultural blinkering, we can learn to attend to shimmers relevant to others.

Theorising shimmers allows me to imagine consumers navigating disparately splintering particles of light, gradients of intensity, sound, shade, colour, arousal, and so on. With bountiful potential knowledges and experience to recognise and process, each consumer of shimmering texts busily assimilates what they can; learns from other refractions of light; enjoys some, rejects or resists further. Such consumption is negotiation – of signs, interpretations, concepts, and feelings – however fleeting or elusive. This is philosophy. The affective quality of shimmers, and the embodied manner through which we enjoy them, means this philosophy is performed throughout our bodies. Cinema consumption involves embodied philosophy.

Signifiance

While an amount of that which is stimulated in our bodies at the cinema we might decode with relative ease using semiotic analysis, many fleeting sensations and intensities of feeling are harder to isolate and translate. They defy conventional discourse. Both sound and sexual arousal (as generated by pornography, for example) have reputations for eluding analysis (Berland 1984; Paasonen 2007). Both also play important roles in the experience of viewing *the Scene* from *Fifty Shades*, generating sensations within consumer-bodies that ostensibly exceed semiotic scrutiny. Kristeva (2000) theorises defiant textual components as *signifiance. Jouissance* – the indescribable pleasure of sex – exemplifies defiance of signification. It also dissolves the perceived boundedness of the self so that consumers "lose" themselves and merge with texts. Deep empathic and affective identification with textual elements thus becomes possible and material meaning is generated. In the context of affective cinematic representations of law, embodied identification potentially informs consumer perceptions of the violence and justice, contract and consent that consumers might take with them from the cinema to shape their experiences of legal ideas beyond.

Signifiance is the inverse of significance (or the conveyance of legible meaning) (Kheshti 2015). This is because *signifiance* "cannot be reduced to . . . communication, representation, expression" (Barthes 1977, 10). It cannot be translated easily into dominant codes of communication, especially when it is felt in the body. However, rather than a-signifying, *signifiance* is meaning-*ful*. The signifying process is made up of significance and *signfiance*. Meaning is produced through the interaction between both. Kristeva (1984) uses music to demonstrate. Music is "nonverbal" and works through the body, defying simple explanation (Rolvjord 2004). Through *signifiance*, music both evokes and conveys emotions that the dominant language cannot normally express. However, music is also created using rules dictating structure, genre, and cultural form – through significance. Rules help differentiate music from noise, musical codes (or signs) have shared meaning within communities and hold political meaning (see Kheshti 2015; Carvahlo 2013). The play of symbolic signs and rules (significance) with emotion and sensation (*signifiance*) in music stretches and manipulates communication structures to express concepts, experiences, and feelings otherwise or previously inexpressible. Significance and *signifiance* shape each other through continual interaction.

The dialectic also manifests in pornography. The central goal of pornography as a genre is to capture and convey that which epitomises resistance to representation: sexual pleasure, orgasm, ecstasy – *jouissance*. The genre attempts to overcome this "representational problem" by stirring reactions in audience bodies (Melendez 2004, 408). Communication of the indescribable requires "a complex nexus of flesh, generic convention, technologies and values" (Paasonen 2010, 67). Signs and signification are what constitute conventions and communicate value while bodily responses are provoked by images, sound, and sensations that we have learnt to recognise and associate with specific ideas communicated without further detailed explanation. In pornography these signs "physically arouse us to meaning" (Sobchack 2004, 57). Thus, affect or *signifiance* and signification/significance are "attached at the hip, sharing . . . vital organs, and detachable only with some degree of violence" (Paasonen 2010, 59). Pornography's excessive and dedicated physical engagement with consumers as arousal exemplifies the interplay of *signifiance* and significance.

Stimulated by sound and pornography, *jouissance* can bring about a *loss of self*. Music is a conduit of *jouissance* as *loss of self*, through which the consumer gives themselves up to the text (Barthes 1977). Music allows consumers to imagine with the whole of their bodies the physical creation of music – including, for example, the *grain of the voice*. Feeling *the grain* resembles the muscle memory activated while watching physical expression as observed by MacDougall (2006). It might be understood as embodied identification. Young (2016) suggests *the grain* enables deep empathy that opens consumers to understand the experience of someone very different from themselves. It may also explain how consumers sometimes enjoy content they might otherwise ideologically oppose. *Loss of self* adds complexity and richness to theories of cinematic identification because it helps to trace the ways in which consumers might be engaged through the whole of their bodies to experiment with the ideas, arguments, and narratives, logic, and ideological structures that are available in even the smallest scenes within a film.

I trace the ways in which *joussiance* is generated through an active *loss of self* – involving the sometimes joyful, sometimes uncomfortable, sometimes rageful, embodied pleasures of consuming cinema. I explore how sound and pornographic conventions encourage us to merge with *the Scene* from *Fifty Shades*. We are supported to *feel* with both characters depicted in the scene, further elements within *the Scene* too. Although this may push us to align our bodies with particular legal arguments presented, we may also and simultaneously practice divergent theories of law through our bodies while watching.

Embodied Cinematic Jurisprudence

Comprehending and enjoying film involves the whole of our diverse bodies. Our bodies are trained in sense-making through an image-based culture, but also throughout our embodied interactions with the intersecting discursive cultures across which we live our daily lives. Our bodies carry knowledge and memory. Part of this knowledge concerns the law. And law "lives in the images that saturate our culture" (Sarat et al. 2005, 1). Consequently, legal ideas circulate through our experiences of going to the cinema and are part of the embodied interpretive practice and philosophy we exercise there.

Young (2010, 122) describes images of crime (the "crime-image") working their affects "under our skin." Young's statement makes my own skin itch. Her affective description materialises bodily engagements with representations of crime. By these means, images influence spectator perceptions and understandings of the wrongness or acceptability of depicted crimes. Consequently, these images inform the audience's expectations of the law.

Buchanan and Johnson (2005, 36) explore the intersection of law and film "in the affective register," investigating how cinematic representations of law and violence elicit sensate responses. Film is a "dynamic process in which we participate as embodied viewers" (Buchanan and Johnson 2008, 39). Through it, we are positioned as audiences "to judge with our whole bodies" when we feel disgust or devastation, pleasure, or excitement towards depictions of violence (Buchanan and Johnson 2005, 56).

Chaudhuri (2014) analyses visceral responses to documentary cinema, particularly those concerning atrocity. These texts are evocative, stirring feelings of righteousness and the need for action in their audiences. But consumers might also come to "give their consent to atrocities or become part of systems of violence" through their physiological engagement with such documentaries (83). That is, through their bodily responses to the textures of a documentary, consumers can be persuaded of the validity of particular instances of violence to accept the politics justifying that violence. Johnson (2009, 822) observes that the "affect-laden power" of screen-based texts often draws us into complicity with law's violence. The sensational seductions of cinema can persuade us of the legitimacy of violence perpetrated in law's name.

It is important to remember that cinematic arguments concerning law's violence often do not align with dominant institutional narratives justifying law. Cinematic texts regularly invite us to think critically about legal practice (Johnson and Buchanan 2001), encourage us to feel uncomfortable about law's authority (Duncanson 2009, 2014), or imagine different forms of justice (Robson 2021). Simultaneously, the layered affective currents of cinematic texts work with complex storylines to provide moments of critique and scepticism about law's legitimacy embedded within otherwise hegemonic overarching plots (Lagerwall 2021, 121). Additionally, consumers do not always comply with preferred or predicted interpretations of screen-based texts.

I argue that individual consumers construct multiple, even dissonant, interpretations of the same piece of cinema, with their whole bodies. They reject, celebrate, and rework lines of logic in a performance of jurisprudence.

Bodies of Philosophy

Although shimmers, *signifiance*, and affects may elude or transcend conventional discourse, they *do* generate meaning as they stir sensations in bodies. Further, embodied meaning-making is philosophical – negotiating concepts and critically engaging with logic. This is because bodily action and experience are not separate from thought. Rather, thought itself is embodied. What is produced through embodied encounters with cinema may be subtle, but it continually informs our subjectivity and our perceptions of the world. This might be understood as *becoming*. And while as embodied subjects we may *become* despite ourselves, we are not passive. When we wrestle with the affects and drives of *becoming*, we wrestle with our fundamental understandings of ourselves and the logic we use to make sense of all that we perceive and experience. This includes law: what law is; legal processes and practices; law's authority. We each practice philosophy with our bodies. Part of what we practice is *legal* philosophy.

The theory of *becoming* refuses dominant understandings of subjectivity as static or bounded – unlike the autonomous and impenetrable sovereign individual of liberal theory. Instead, *becoming* understands us to function like the feet of a gecko. Geckos can climb any surface (except Teflon) upside-down using molecular interaction (Autumn and Puthoff 2016). Contrasting mechanical interlocking adhesion systems, gecko feet use intermolecular forces to mingle with a surface's molecules or bonded groups of atoms. At the smallest measurable unit, gecko feet *become* part of the surface. *Becoming* theory understands that we also *become* part of what we touch or with what we interact. The distinctions between all things (human and non-human bodies, atmospheres, and so on) are blurred and can fold into each other. Each "human body is radically open to its surroundings and can be composed, recomposed and decomposed by other bodies" (Gatens 1996, 110). Like the gecko scuttling over the ceiling, we might appear contained and bounded – we might "stick" but are not stuck. However, we are mixing with other matter and always becoming towards, are influenced by, that other matter. We are always changing in relation to all that we brush up against: we are "always becoming otherwise, however subtly" (Gregg and Seigworth 2010, 3). This is to understand ourselves as bodies – the very matter of who we are – as a "process always underway rather than a position taken" (4). We never arrive as a finished product or an essential self, even though culturally we work on the basis that each person has a "true/essential/authentic" self. Nor is our ideological alignment static, but always fluctuating. Relatedly, our logic and frameworks of understanding are always in process, they are dissonant, self-contradicting, vacillating between opposing perspectives: inconsistent. Legal ideas are woven through this embodiment, inflecting our *becomings* but also interpreting legal ideas while folding them into different material forms and beings.

Becoming is embodied subjectivity in flow or motion, stimulated and informed by affect. Simultaneously, affects "make us feel, write, think, and act in different ways" (Probyn in Gregg and Steigworth 2010, 14). These acts might be manifestations of becoming. Affect, becoming, embodied subjectivity and thought are interconnected. As affect stimulates becoming, so it also shapes thought. Or rather, affect *is* thought, because "affect and cognition are never fully separable" (2). Gregg and Steigworth (2) describe "sensate tendrils" as constantly extending between non-conscious affect and conscious thought. For Braidotti (1991, 165) "all knowledge rests on libidinal . . . affective and corporeal grounds." Thought is embodied; the practice of reason and the generation of knowledge is performed by and through bodies (Gatens 1996, 110).

While we are constantly *becoming*, we are also endlessly interpreting and making sense of conventional signification as well as *affect*, *signifiance*, and *shimmers*. Neither signification nor *signifiance* are stable. Neither signs nor affects signify or mean anything prior to apprehension and assimilation. Meaning does not pre-exist, is not stable, inherent, transcendent, nor a-priori. Meaning only exists in the moment of meaning-making. It depends on our interpretative labour. That labour is constant because of "the infinity of little affective events that make up our everyday lives" (Gregg and Siegworth 2010, 15). Thus, *becoming* involves endless interpretive activity.

In cinemas, consumers are continuously working to make sense of what they consume, to grasp and still shimmers so they can assimilate them into pre-existing but also ever-changing discourses and schemas. This work is not only cognitive but exercised by the whole of the body of the consumer. In the activity of embodied interpretation, the consumer is also shifting and changing themselves and their philosophy, their interpretation of the world . . . and of law.

Film viewing can therefore be appreciated as an activity involving the processing of multisensorial stimuli by each consumer, as they grapple with affects, refracting light, and fleeting sensations. Each consumer is individually trained or enculturated through prior experiences and *becomings* to generate logical narratives that make sense to them, assimilating what they consume and feel. This labour is about generating something out of the offered stimuli, which is ostensibly logical and believable. This is philosophy: processing information and assimilating it into already existing knowledge. But also adapting those ideas and frameworks because the constant encounters provide new angles and perspectives in a manner that might be understood as endless *becoming*. Through our ceaselessly morphing interpretation of the world, our subjectivity also alters, however slightly.

When a scene holds a contract at its heart, the embodied philosophical labour is jurisprudential. It involves processing legal theory and assimilating in/accurate legal knowledge into the materiality of enjoying (or not) *the Scene* in *Fifty Shades*. The central purpose of this book is to prove that consumers are physically theorising law and generating legal meaning while at the cinema.

Fifty Shades of Grey

Later, I demonstrate how the sheer extent of popular consumption of *Fifty Shades*, as well as the related controversy, is a significant justification for using it as a case study for investigating popular jurisprudence at the cinema. As an "erotic" romance, the film is also rich with examples of the way in which consumer-bodies are engaged with legal ideas. This is because *Fifty Shades* combines genres openly recognised as arousing sensation while its narrative is preoccupied with a contract. But first, the basic narrative:

Fifty Shades begins with an awkwardly shy college student, Anastasia Steele (Ana), compelled to interview millionaire entrepreneur Christian Grey. She literally stumbles into his office and there is instant attraction. Through a series of coincidental and engineered (by Christian) encounters, the two are drawn together. It is revealed that while Ana is a sexually awakening virgin, Christian is considerably experienced. More precisely, his traumatic childhood predisposes him to contractual dominant/submissive arrangements, with him exerting absolute control over women's lives. Negotiations start between Ana and Christian when Christian insists he cannot have a "vanilla" relationship and requires Ana to contract herself into a submissive role. Ana resists, but wavers. She considers the contract and its list of acts, toys, and rules to which she would be consenting. At the same time, she petitions him to contemplate a more romantic relationship. In between, the couple has sex many times, engaging in some BDSM, both crossing their own boundaries – often without verbal negotiation, but always with orgasmic outcome. Eventually, Ana refuses to sign the contract and ends the relationship. The last shot of the film is Christian unable to focus on a business meeting.

The movie is the first adaptation of a sensationally consumed book trilogy. As such, most of its consumers are aware of the overarching plot across the three novels. The trilogy concludes after the couple marry with an epilogue showing them with a toddler and Ana pregnant. I approach my analysis of *Fifty Shades* with an assumption that consumers know Ana and Christian ultimately marry and have children.

The film was immensely successful. The book was the "fastest-selling paperback since records began [and the] first ebook to sell more than one million copies" (Thorpe 2012). Illouz (2014, 8) situates the trilogy "among some of the best-selling series in all of modern publishing." The film set several US box office records including the greatest takings for a Valentine's Day opening (Gray 2015), best opening weekend for a female director (McClintock 2015), and best overseas opening weekend for an R-rated film

(Tartaglione 2015). It was the fourth highest-grossing female-directed film, and highest-grossing R-rated film of all time (Mendelson 2015a, 2015b). The film's presumed consumers are women, and its impressive earnings are due to its triumph in satisfying a very significant proportion of Anglophile populations across the West.

This success attests to the film being enjoyed by a substantial proportion of a large cultural community. Illouz (2014, 7) identifies best-sellers for their "capacity to capture values and outlooks that are either dominant and widely institutionalised or widespread enough to become mainstreamed by a cultural medium." The film version of *Fifty Shades* is an instance of shared understanding: the array of signifiers (images, sounds, narratives, sensations) that make up the text are extensively recognised across a mildly variegated array of predominantly English-speaking cultures. For Thorpe (2012), the phenomenon represents a shared fantasy. I am interested in some of the less overtly discursive ideas present in the film which shape the shared fantasies and that both concern law *and* make the film comprehensible and enjoyable for its vast audience.

Fifty Shades' fierce popularity is controversial. Both the books and films have been dismissed in classed and gendered terms as badly written "mummy porn" (Dymock 2013, 883; McCann 2015). Throughout much of the plentiful popular, critical, and academic discussions Dymock observes that "the idea of taking *Fifty Shades* seriously . . . has . . . been ridiculed . . . alongside near-universal denouncement of its 'terrible writing'" (Dymock 2013, 880). Most commentary Deller and Smith (2013, 935) surveyed could "barely conceal . . . contempt." The books have been condemned as damaging and "dangerous" to readers (Whitehead 2013; Thorpe 2012; Purcell 2013). Predominantly, there appears to be an inverse relationship between the mass appeal of *Fifty Shades* and feminist "approval."

Meanwhile, some feminists have sought to appreciate the worth in *Fifty Shades*, particularly to avoid condemnation of its large, primarily female, audience (Deller and Smith 2013). It is praised for allowing greater female ownership of sexual fantasy and "for raising the subject of female sexuality" (Dymock 2013, 884). Similarly, Illouz (2014, 6) argues that *Fifty Shades* "represents the ultimate triumph of a female point of view in culture," while Jones and Mills (2014) document its female readers' sense of empowerment.

The controversy demonstrates that manifold interpretations of the text are available. The multiple interpretations, conflicting mass readership and critical condemnation, together with a documented ambivalence of reader attitudes, evidence reader agency. Such complex engagements with *Fifty Shades* are central to my argument that consumers of the film actively negotiate ideas while they are at the cinema. For this reason, *Reader Agency* concerns the agentic practices of consumers of "women's fiction." Ultimately, in the third reading, my interest lies in the moments when these ideas concern law and engage consumers' bodies.

In addition to the film's relevance as an indicative cultural text of engaged consumption, the film is also pertinent to my argument due to the explicitly visceral nature of its genre. As a pornographic romance, *Fifty Shades* sits across two genres often deplored for their effect on bodies. Pornography is created with the distinct purpose of sexual arousal (Williams 2005). Arousal is "an index of [porn's] marginalisation" (10–11). It is also a concern of law, with law and policy makers worried about the possible harm pornography inflicts upon its aroused viewers, and through their apparently toxic arousal, the harm they might perpetrate against others (Williams 1999, 186). Correspondingly, romantic films are cast as low culture because they illicit easy tears and joy from their targeted women consumers. Further, romance shares pornography's commitment to generating embodied arousal (Snitow in Paasonen 2018). What makes *Fifty Shades* both pornography *and* romance is what also makes it a very affective cinematic experience. The elements it shares with these genres are those that reach out to affect consumer-bodies. Thus, its sensually encoded discourse makes it an ideal text for answering my research questions.

Ultimately, it is the centrality of a contract that renders *Fifty Shades* so compelling to me. Much of the film's sexual tension derives from Ana's indecision about signing a contract. Although it is not legally binding, this contract uses legal language, and its terms echo the power structure of former marriage contracts. At the same time, as a sexually explicit romance, *Fifty Shades* is haunted by contemporary arguments about legitimate sex and consent, that kernel of rape law. Woven through the romantic narrative and pornographic aesthetics, various conceptualisations of contract and consent become part of the carnal experience of watching intimacy on screen. This sensual material illustrates how viewing bodies are physically engaged in theorising law at the cinema.

The configuration of the film's contract as establishing a "sub/dom" relationship as part of bondage and discipline, dominance and submission, and sadomasochist (BDSM) practices is important to note. BDSM is recognised as part of the appeal of *Fifty Shades* and justifies the centrality of the contract, with the contract being a commonly assumed aspect of BDSM culture. Although exploration of the film's representation of BDSM offers another array of perspectives, it also brings a bundle of concerns requiring careful navigation and expertise in BDSM. Numerous critics and scholars have criticised *Fifty Shades* as not correctly representing BDSM (Beres and MacDonald 2015; Tsaros 2013; Barker 2013). Meanwhile, Boyle (2018) argues that the BDSM in *Fifty Shades* acts as an "alibi" for Christian's violence – authorising it by situating it within a popular narrative of pathologised trauma and sub/dom desire. Separately, despite the emphasis on contract in BDSM culture, coercion and violence still occur (Barker 2013). Tyler and Tarzia (2015) insist that BDSM exists on a continuum of violence. For these reasons, it is negligent to dismiss concerns about violence in *Fifty Shades* on the basis of an explicit contract. Analysing *Fifty Shades* through a BDSM lens offers compelling insights, but also raises complex tensions requiring deeper explorations that diverge from the central purpose of my book. Ultimately, while BDSM culture is often celebrated as demonstrating the empowerment and efficacy of contracts for navigating the complexity of shared pain and pleasure crossing lines of legally sanctioned and forbidden harm, the contract in *Fifty Shades* remains plagued by the same problems that make the primacy of consent in rape law a point of dispute between feminists.

In this book, I focus on a single scene from *Fifty Shades*. This is the climactic contract scene, a mock boardroom meeting in which Ana and Christian negotiate the contract. I call it *the Scene*. It can be found as a YouTube video using "*Fifty Shades of Grey*" and "The Meeting."

After an interlude reflecting on watching the related film series *Twilight* with my friends during COVID lockdowns, *Reader Agency* establishes the agency of consumers and, particularly, the sophisticated labour exercised by consumers of "women's fiction." An interlude describes *the Scene* in detail so that I can more easily present my liberal feminist legal reading in *First Reading: The Frisson of Sexual Agency*. This chapter establishes the presence of law and legal theory in *the Scene*. The post-structuralist feminist legal interpretation in *Second Reading: The Discomforts of Subordination* demonstrates that there is more than one legal theory available in the text. As a single consumer and theorist reading *the Scene* in two ways, I propose that others also pick up divergent threads of legal philosophy, evaluate them and generate their own unique interpretation of the film and its law. In *Third Reading 1: Legal Sensations Between Orgasms* I focus on the shimmers and *signifiance* of *the Scene's* sound and pornographic conventions as they potentially generate a *loss of self* and stir empathic engagement in ways that might shape consumers' embodied engagement with legal ideas. I return to consumer agency in *Third Reading 2: Doing Jurisprudence with Your Body* to show how the embodied engagement with *the Scene* is a performance of legal philosophy. This is how I understand consumers practice jurisprudence with their bodies at the cinema. In my *Postlude*, I suggest that embodied jurisprudence is performed beyond cinemas in the most ordinary, intimate, and desire-driven activities such that we might be able to conceive of sex jurisprudentially.

Bibliography

Ahmed, Sara. (2007). Multiculturalism and the Promise of Happiness. *New Formations*, 63(1), pp. 121–137.

Autumn, Kellar, and Puthoff, Jonathan. (2016). Properties, Principles and Parameters of the Gecko Adhesive System. In Smith, Andrew (Ed). *Biological Adhesives* (2nd ed., pp. 245–280). Springer International Publishing. https://doi.org/10.1007/978-3-319-46082-6_11

Baird, Barbara. (2006). Sexual Citizenship in "the New Tasmania". *Political Geography*, 25(8), pp. 964–987.

Barker, Meg. (2013). Consent is a Grey Area? A Comparison of Understandings of Consent in *Fifty Shades of Grey* and on the BDSM Blogosphere. *Sexualities*, 16(8), pp. 896–914.

Barthes, Roland. (1977). *Image, Music, Text* (Heath, Stephen Trans). Noonday Press.

Barthes, Roland. (2005). *The Neutral* (Krauss, Rosalind E., and Hollier, Denis Trans.). Columbia University Press.

Beres, Melanie, and MacDonald, Jo. (2015). Talking About Sexual Consent. *Australian Feminist Studies*, 30(86), pp. 418–432.

Berland, Jody. (Fall, 1984). Contradicting Media: Toward a Political Phenomenology of Listening. *Border/Lines*, pp. 32–36.

Bloodsworth-Lugo, Mary K., and Lugo-Lugo, Carmen R. (2010). *Containing (un)*American Bodies: Race, *Sexuality and Post-9/11 Constructions of Citizenship*. Brill/Rodopi Press.

Boyle, Karen. (2018). The Implications of Pornification: Pornography, the Mainstream and False Equivalences. In Lombard, Nancy (Ed). *The Routledge Handbook of Gender and Violence* (1st ed., pp. 85–96). Routledge.

Braidotti, Rosie. (1991). *Patterns of Dissonance: A Study of Women and Contemporary Philosophy* (Guild, Elizabeth Trans.). Polity Press.

Buchanan, Ruth, and Johnson, Rebecca. (2005). The Unforgiven Sources of International Law: Nation-building, Violence, and Gender in the West(ern). In Buss, Doris, and Manji, Ambreena (Eds). *International Law: Modern Feminist Approaches* (pp. 135–158). Hart Publishing.

Buchanan, Ruth, and Johnson, Rebecca. (2008). Strange Encounters: Exploring Law and Film in the Affective Register. *Studies in Law, Politics and Society*, 46, pp. 33–60.

Campbell, Fiona A. (1999). "Refleshingly Disabled": Interrogations into the Corporeality of "Disabled" Bodies. *Australian Feminist Law Journal*, 12(1), pp. 57–80.

Carline, Anna, Gunby, Clare, and Murray, Jamie. (2021). "And that's Why Street-Wise Complainants Now Always Give Evidence Behind Screens, Live": Exploring the Intensive Affects of the Courtroom. In Duncanson, Kirsty, and Henderson, Emma (Eds). *Courthouse Architecture, Design and Social Justice* (pp. 169–190). Routledge.

Carvahlo, John. (2013). "Strange Fruit": Music Between Silence and Death. *The Journal of Aesthetics and Art Criticism*, 71(1), pp. 111–119.

Chaudhuri, Shohini. (2014). *Cinema of the Dark Side: Atrocity and the Ethics of Film Spectatorship*. Edinburgh University Press.

Clark, Anna. (1996). Gender, Class and the Constitution: Franchise Reform in England 1832–1928. In Vernon, James (Ed). *Re-Reading the Constitution: New Narratives in the Political History of England's Long Nineteenth Century* (pp. 239–253). Cambridge University Press.

Collis, Christy, and Bainbridge, Jason. (2005). Introduction – Popular Cultures and the Law. *Continuum*, 19(2), pp. 159–164.

Corbett v Corbett (Otherwise Ashley) [1970] 2 All E.R. 33.

Cover, Robert. (1986). Violence and the Word. *Yale Law Journal*, 95, pp. 1601–1625.

Cowan, Sharon. (2007). Choosing Freely: Theoretically Reframing the Concept of Consent. In Hunter, Rosemary, and Cowan, Sharon (Eds). *Choice and Consent: Feminist Engagements with Law and Subjectivity* (pp. 91–105). Routledge-Cavendish.

Crawley, Karen. (2016). The Critical Force of Irony: Reframing Photographs in Cultural Legal Studies. In Leiboff, Marett, and Sharp, Cassandra (Eds). *Cultural Legal Studies: Law's Popular Cultures and the Metamorphosis of Law* (pp. 183–205). Routledge.

Crenshaw, Kimberlé Williams. (1994). Mapping the Margins: Intersectionality, Identity Politics, and Violence Against Women of Color. In Fineman, Martha, and Mytikiuk, Roxanne (Eds). *The Public Nature of Private Violence* (pp. 93–119). Routledge.

D'Cruz, Carolyn. (2020). *Democracy in Difference: Debating Key Terms of Gender, Sexuality, Race and Identity*. La Trobe University Press.

Del Rio, Elena. (2000). The Body of Voyeurism: Mapping a Discourse of the Senses in Michael Powell's *Peeping Tom*. *Camera Obscura*, 15(3), pp. 115–149.

Deller, Ruth A., and Smith, Clarissa. (2013). Reading the BDSM Romance: Reader Responses to *Fifty Shades*. *Sexualities*, 16(8), pp. 932–950.

Duncanson, Kirsty. (2009). The Scene of the Crime: The Uneasy Figuring of Anglo-Australian Sovereignty in the Landscape of 'Lantana'. *Law Text Culture*, 13, pp. 25–54.

Duncanson, Kirsty. (2014). "Native" Landscapes, "Cultivated" Gardens and the Erasure of Indigenous Sovereignty in Two Recent Instances of Australian Cinematic Popular Jurisprudential Imagining. *Law, Culture and the Humanities*, 10, pp. 237–256.

Duncanson, Kirsty. (2020). Being Engaged in Colonial Critique by Mojo Juju's 'Native Tongue.' In Tranter, Kieran, Weinert, Kim, and Crawley, Karen (Eds). *Law, Lawyers and Justice: Through Australian Lenses* (pp. 144–175). Routledge.

Duncanson, Kirsty, and Emma Henderson. (2014). Narrative, Theatre and the Disruptive Potential of Jury Directions in Rape Trials. *Feminist Legal Studies*, 22, pp. 155–174.

Dymock, Alex. (2013). Flogging Sexual Transgression: Interrogating the Costs of the '*Fifty Shades* Effect'. *Sexualities*, 16(8), pp. 880–895.

Elander, Maria. (2014). Education and Photography at Tuol Sleng Genocide Museum. In Rush, Peter, and Simić, Olivera (Eds). *The Arts of Transitional Justice: Culture, Activism and Memory After Atrocity* (pp. 43–62). Springer.

Ellison, Louise, and Munro, Vanessa. (2009). Reacting to Rape: Exploring Mock Jurors' Assessments of Complainant Credibility. *British Journal of Criminology*, 49(2), pp. 202–219.

Gatens, Moira. (1996). *Imaginary Bodies: Ethics, Power and Corporeality*. Routledge.

Giddens, Thomas. (2015). *Graphic Justice: Intersections of Comics and Law*. Routledge.

Grabham, Emily. (2009). Shaking Mr Jones: Law and Touch. *International Journal of Law in Context*, 5(4). pp. 343–353.

Gray, Brandon. (February 16, 2015). Weekend Report: Valentine's Day Massacres Presidents' Day Record. *Box Office Mojo*. www.boxofficemojo.com/article/ed2658796548/

Green, Richard. (2001). (Serious) Sadomasochism: A Protected Right of Privacy? *Archives of Sexual Behavior*, 30(5), pp. 543–550.

Greenfield, Steve, Osborne, Guy, and Robson, Peter. (2010). *Film and the Law: The Cinema Justice*. Hart Publishing.

Gregg, Melissa, and Seigworth, Gregory. (2010). *The Affects Theory Reader*. Duke University Press.

Gunby, Clare, and Carline, Anna. (2020). The Emotional Particulars of Working on Rape Cases: Doing Dirty Work, Managing Emotional Dirt and Conceptualizing 'Tempered Indifference.' *The British Journal of Criminology*, 60(2), pp. 343–362.

Gunning, Tom. (1990). The Cinema of Attractions: Early Cinema, Its Spectator and the Avant Garde. In Elsaesser, Thomas (Ed). *Early Cinema: Space, Frame, Narrative* (pp. 56–62). British Film Institute.

Hamilton, Sheryl, Majury, Diana, Moore, Dawn, Sargent, Neil, and Wilke, Christiane. (2016). *Sensing Law*. Taylor and Francis.

Hanich, Julian. (2018). *The Audience Effect: On the Collective Cinema Experience*. Edinburgh University Press.

Hanna, Charyl. (2000–2001). Sex is Not a Sport: Consent and Violence in Criminal Law. *Boston College Law Review*, 42, pp. 239–290.

Howes, David. (2019). Prologue: Introduction to Sensori-Legal Studies. *Canadian Journal of Law and Society*, 34(2), pp. 173–189.

Iedema, Rick. (2021). *Affected: On Becoming Undone and Potentiation*. Springer International Publishing.

Illouz, Eva. (2014). *Hard-Core Romance: Fifty Shades of Grey, Best Sellers and Society*. University of Chicago Press.

Ison, Jess. (2020). "It's Not Just Men and Women": LGBTQIA People and #MeToo'. In Loney-Howes, Rachel, and Fileborn, Bianca (Eds). *#MeToo and the Politics of Social Change* (pp. 151–167). Palgrave MacMillan.

Johnson, Rebecca. (2009). Living *Deadwood*: Imagination, Affect, and the Persistence of the Past. *Suffolk University Law Review*, 42(4), pp. 809–828.

Johnson, Rebecca, and Buchanan, Ruth. (2001). Getting the Insider's Story Out: What Popular Film Can Tell Us about Legal Method's Dirty Secrets. *The Windsor Yearbook of Access to Justice = Recueil Annuel De Windsor D'accès à La Justice*, 20, p. 87.

Jones, Lucy, and Mills, Sara. (2014). Analysing Agency: Reader Responses to *Fifty Shades of Grey*. *Gender and Language*, 8(2), pp. 225–244.

Kamler, Barbara, and Maclean, Rod. (1997). "You Can't Just Go to Court and Move Your Body": First-Year Law Students Learn to Write and Speak the Law. *Law, Text, Culture*, 3(1), pp. 176–209.

Kheshti, Roshanak. (2015). *Modernity's Ear: Listening to Race and Gender in World Music*. New York University Press.

Kristeva, Julia. (1984). *Revolution in Poetic Language* (Waller, Margaret Trans.). Columbia University Press.

Kristeva, Julia. (2000). *The Sense and Non-Sense of Revolt: The Powers and Limits of Psychoanalysis* (Herman, Jeanine Trans.). Columbia University Press.

Lagerwall, Anne. (2021). Is Cinema the Handmaid of International Criminal Justice? In Corten, Olivier, Dubuisson, François, and Falkowsla-Clarys, Martyna (Eds). *Cinematic Perspectives on International Law* (pp. 104–127). Manchester University Press.

Leiboff, Marett. (2015). Towards a Jurisprudence of the Embodied Mind-Sarah Lund, Forbrydelsen and the Mindful Body. *Naveiñ Reet: Nordic Journal of Law and Social Research (NNJLSR)*, 6, p. 77.

Leiboff, Marett, and Sharp, Cassandra. (2016). Cultural Legal Studies and Law's Popular Cultures. In Leiboff, Marett, and Sharp, Cassandra (Eds). *Cultural Legal Studies: Law's Popular Cultures and the Metamorphosis of Law* (pp. 1–28). Routledge.

MacDougall, David. (2006). *The Corporeal Image: Film, Ethnography and the Senses*. Princeton University Press.

MacNeil, William. (1998). Law's *Corpus Delecti*: The Fantasmatic Body of Rights Discourse. *Law and Critique*, 9(1), pp. 37–57.

MacNeil, William. (2007). *Lex Populi: The Jurisprudence of Popular Culture*. Stanford University Press.

Manderson, Desmond. (2003). From Hunger to Love: Myths of Sources, Interpretation, and Constitution of Law in Children's Literature. *Law and Literature*, 15(1), pp. 87–141.

Manderson, Desmond, and Turner, Sarah. (2006). Coffee House: *Habitus* and the Performance Among Law Students. *Law and Social Inquiry*, 31(3), pp. 649–676.

McCann, Hannah. (February 18, 2015). The 'Mommy Porn' Myth: Who are the Fifty Shades of Grey Fans? *The Conversation*. https://theconversation.com/the-mommy-porn-myth-who-are-the-fifty-shades-of-grey-fans-37649

McClintock, Pamela. (February 15, 2015). *Fifty Shades* Scores Biggest Opening in History for a Female Director. *The Hollywood Reporter*. www.hollywoodreporter.com/news/general-news/fifty-shades-scores-biggest-opening-773601/

Melendez, Franklin. (2004). Video Pornography, Visual Pleasure. In Williams, Linda (Ed). *Porn Studies* (pp. 401–428). Duke University Press.

Mendelson, Scott. (February 19, 2015a). Box Office: *Fifty Shades of Grey* Tops $100M US, $300 WorldWide. *Forbes*. www.forbes.com/sites/scottmendelson/2015/02/19/box-office-fifty-shades-of-grey-tops-100m-us-300m-worldwide/

Mendelson, Scott. (March 5, 2015b). Box Office: *Fifty Shades of Grey* Becomes 6th R-Rated Film to Top $500M. *Forbes*. www.forbes.com/sites/scottmendelson/2015/03/05/box-office-fifty-shades-becomes-6th-r-rated-film-to-top-500m/

Moran, Leslie. (2002). *The Homosexual(ity) of Law*. Routledge.

Moran, Leslie J., Sandon, Emma, Loizidou, Elena, and Christie, Ian. (2004). Introduction. In Moran, Leslie J., Sandon, Emma, Loizidou, Elena, and Christie, Ian (Eds). *Law's Moving Image*. Glass House Press.

Moraru, Christian. (2016). "Neutrality" as Nomos?: Paradigm, Nuance, and the Politics of Coterritoriality in Late Barthes. *The Comparatist*, 40(1), pp. 284–298.

Morgan, Wayne. (1993–1994). Identifying Evil for What It is: Tasmania, Sexual Perversity and the United Nations. *Melbourne University Law Review*, 19, pp. 740–757.
Munro, Vanessa. (2008). Constructing Consent: Legislating Freedom and Legitimating Constraint in the Expression of Sexual Autonomy. *Akron Law Review*, 41, pp. 923–956.
NSW Registrar v Norrie 2014 250 CLR 490.
Ott, Brian. (2010). The Visceral Politics of *V for Vendetta*: On Political Affect in Cinema. *Critical Studies in Media Communication*, 27(1), pp. 39–54.
Paasonen, Susanna. (2007). Strange Bedfellows: Pornography, Affect and Feminist Reading. *Feminist Theory*, 8(1), pp. 43–57.
Paasonen, Susanna. (2010). Disturbing, Fleshy Texts: Close Looking at Pornography. In Paasonen, Susanna, and Liljeström, Marianne (Eds). *Working with Affect in Feminist Readings: Disturbing Differences* (pp. 58–71). Taylor and Francis.
Paasonen, Susanna. (2018). Many Splendored Things: Sexuality, Playfulness and Play. *Sexualities*, 21(4), pp. 537–551.
Patterson, Jennifer. (2016). *Queering Sexual Violence: Radical Voices from within the Anti-Violence Movement*. Riverdale Avenue Books.
Philippopoulos-Mihalopoulos, Andreas. (2013). Atmospheres of Law: Senses, Affects, Lawscapes. *Emotion, Space and Society*, 7, pp. 35–44.
Podlas, Kimberly. (2008). Guilty by All Accounts: *Law and Order*'s Impact on Public Perceptions of Law and Order. *Seton Hall Journal of Sports and Entertainment Law*, 18, pp. 1–18.
Purcell, Carey. (March 4, 2013). *Fifty Shades of Feminism – a Response to E. L. James* [Blog Post]. www.careypurcell.com/articles/8141
Razack, Sherene. (1994). From Consent to Responsibility, from Pity to Respect: Subtexts in Cases of Sexual Violence Involving Girls and Women with Developmental Disabilities. *Law & Social Inquiry*, 19(4), pp. 891–922.
Robson, P. W. G. (2021). Developments in Revenge, Justice and Rape in the Cinema. *International Journal for the Semiotics of Law*, 34, pp. 69–88.
Rogers, Juliet. (2003). Making the Crimes (Female Genital Mutilation) Act 1996, Making the (Non) Mutilated Woman. *Australian Feminist Law Journal*, 18(1), pp. 93–114.
Rolvjord, Randi. (2004). Music as a Poetic Language. *Voices: A World Forum for Music Therapy*, 4(1), no pages.
Ryan, Tess. (2020). This Black Body is Not Yours for the Taking. In Loney-Howes, Rachel, and Fileborn, Bianca (Eds). *#MeToo and the Politics of Social Change* (pp. 117–132). Palgrave MacMillan.
Salzman, Victoria, and Dunwoody, Philip. (2005). Prime Time Lies: Do Portrayals of Lawyers Influence How People Think about the Legal Profession. *Southern Methodist University Law Review*, 58, pp. 411–464.
Sarat, Austin, Douglas, Lawrence, and Umphrey, Martha Merrill. (2005). On Film and Law: Broadening the Focus. In Sarat, Austin, Douglas, Lawrence, and Umphrey, Martha Merrill (Eds). *Law on the Screen* (pp. 1–24). Stanford University Press. https://doi.org/10.1515/9780804767675-003
Saussure, Ferdinand De. (2013). *Course in General Linguistics* (Harris, Roy Trans.). Bloomsbury Publishing.

Sharp, Cassandra. (2016). Finding Stories if Justice in the Art of Conversation: Ethnography in Cultural Legal Studies. In Leiboff, Marett, and Sharp, Cassandra (Eds). *Cultural Legal Studies: Law's Popular Cultures and the Metamorphosis of Law* (pp. 50–67). Routledge.

Sherwin, Richard. (2000). *When Law Goes Pop*. University of Chicago Press.

Skarlicki, Daniel P., Hoegg, JoAndrea, Acquino, Karl, and Nadisic, Thierry. (2013). Does Injustice Affect Your Sense of Taste and Smell? The Mediating Role of Moral Disgust. *Journal of Experimental Social Psychology*, 49(5), pp. 852–859.

Sobchack, Vivian Carol. (1992). *The Address of the Eye: A Phenomenology of Film Experience*. Princeton University Press.

Sobchack, Vivian Carol. (2004). *Carnal Thoughts: Embodiment and Moving Image Culture*. University of California Press.

Steinbock, Eliza. (2019). *Shimmering Images: Trans Cinema, Embodiment, and the Aesthetics of Change*. Duke University Press.

Tartaglione, Nancy. (February 17, 2015). "*Fifty Shades*" Higher in Global Bow At $266.6M; Record R-Rated Opening Overseas – Tuesday Update. *Deadline.com*. https://deadline.com/2015/02/fifty-shades-of-grey-international-box-office-first-day-1201372179/

Taylor-Johnson, Samantha (Director). (2015). *Fifty Shades of Grey* [Film] Focus Features, Michael De Luca Productions, Trigger Street Productions, Universal Pictures.

Thorpe, Vanessa. (July 1, 2012). Why Does Fifty Shades of Grey Turn British Women on? *The Guardian*. www.theguardian.com/books/2012/jun/30/fifty-shades-grey-women-sadomasochism

Tranter, Kieran. (2012). Come a Day There Won't Be Room for Naughty Men Like Us to Slop About at All: The Multi-Media Outlaws of Serenity and the Possibilities of Post-Literate Justice. *Law Text Culture*, 16, pp. 277–304.

Tsaros, Angelika. (2013). Consensual Non-consent: Comparing EL James's *Fifty Shades of Grey* and Pauline Réage's. *Story of O*" *Sexualities*, 16(8), pp. 864–879.

Tyler, Meagan, and Tarzia, Laura. (February 13, 2015). Violence Dressed Up as Erotica: Fifty Shades of Grey and Abuse. *The Conversation*. https://theconversation.com/violence-dressed-up-as-erotica-fifty-shades-of-grey-and-abuse-37589

Whitehead, Deborah. (2013). When Religious 'Mommy Bloggers' Met 'Mommy Porn': Evangelical and Mormon Women's Responses to *Fifty Shades*. *Sexualities*, 16(8). pp. 915–931.

Williams, Linda Ruth. (1999). *Hard Core: Power, Pleasure and the 'Frenzy of the Visible'*. University of California Press.

Williams, Linda Ruth. (2005). *The Erotic Thriller in Contemporary Cinema*. Indiana University Press.

Williams, Linda Ruth. (2008). *Screening Sex*. Duke University Press.

Young, Alison. (2005). *Judging the Image: Art, Value, Law*. Routledge.

Young, Alison. (2010). *The Scene of Violence: Cinema Crime Affect*. Routledge.

Young, Miriam. (2016). *Singing the Body Electric: The Human Voice and Sound Technology*. Routledge.

Interlude – *Twilight Delight*

For five Sunday nights during Lockdown 2.0, Melbourne (Australia) 2020, I sat on my sofa trying to keep up with a WhatsApp chat we called "Twilight Delight" while following the teen vampire romance unfolding on my TV screen. My friends and I watched the cinematic adaptations of the *Twilight* novels (Hardwicke 2008; Weitz 2009; Slade 2010; Condon 2011, 2012) separately but synchronously from our homes scattered across the city. The *Twilight Saga* (Meyer 2005, 2006, 2007, 2008) was a direct inspiration for *Fifty Shades of Grey* (James 2012; Morrison 2012). Watching in conversation with my friends made me think a lot about how predominantly female audiences consume their chosen films.

Our WhatsApp feed resonates with pleasure in the sexual tension between *Twilight's* heroine, Bella, and her love interests Edward and Jacob. There is an appreciation of the vampire aesthetic and actor Kristen Stewart. We gossip about celebrities and comment on subplots and supporting characters. There is sarcasm and humour, exclamations of delight over actors, costumes and soundtrack, emoji eye-rolls over camera angles, dialogue, animation, and special effects. We give relationship advice to Bella. Bella's father is gushed over. Individual friends take breaks to avoid triggering content while others express horror, rage, disgust, and incredulity at colonial narratives, submissive femininity, toxic masculinity, and neoliberal patriarchy.

When my friends type about the hero's romantic actions in terms of gendered violence, their criticism of the film echoes feminist informed law reform that finally views following a person, turning up at their home regularly without invitation, tampering with vehicles and breaking into their bedroom to watch them sleep to be criminal harms. We also talk about behaviour we feel should be prevented through law and public education. Meanwhile, the thrill any of us share in the film's representation of these acts as romantic aligns with gendered violence as cultural tropes of romance both in fiction and law. My friends worry about the film's representation of legal parenthood and its reliance on narratives echoing the law's justifications for colonial land acquisition and First Nations dispossession. Legal ideas are explicit in our commentary, largely because some of us are socio-legal scholars. But our

DOI: 10.4324/9780429330414-3

unambiguous identification of law only makes its presence in the text unambiguous, where otherwise it is indirect.

Our tone is mostly amused. We laugh at ourselves because as tertiary educated feminists, we *know* our enjoyment of *Twilight* is "wrong." Our amusement also derives from our mocking criticism of the films as "bad." There is pleasure in analysing them. We enjoy pulling them apart, scoffing, ridiculing, analysing, being outraged. We indulge in our own cleverness. We love hating the films just as we also love them.

The interwoven threads of our collaborative viewing resemble consumption practices at the heart of this book. Anecdotally, they replicate many of the skills I survey in the chapter on "Reader Agency as Philosophy", that feminist research observes performed with dexterity by consumers of women's fiction. Our *twilight delight* evidences the efforts we each exert to decode film; analyse cinematic aesthetic and narrative form; identify with multiple characters and scenarios; reflect on our own experiences in relation to representation; and generate pleasure through active engagement with both the films and other people. Together, my friends and I are evidence that *Twilight* is not just fodder for the passive enjoyment of unsophisticated audiences. Instead, we are proof that the joys of consuming such texts can be about simultaneously loving and loving to hate them. Particularly important, the chat contains multiple and dissonant interpretations which are constructed through critical and reflective thought. We are performing theory, we are practicing philosophy, we are enacting jurisprudence.

Bibliography

Condon, Bill (Director). (2011). *The Twilight Saga: Breaking Dawn, Part 1* [Film] USA: Summit Entertainment.

Condon, Bill (Director). (2012). *The Twilight Saga: Breaking Dawn, Part 2* [Film] USA: Summit Entertainment.

Hardwicke, Catherine (Director). (2008). *Twilight* [Film] USA: Summit Entertainment, Temple Hill Entertainment.

James, E. L. (2012). *Fifty Shades of Grey*. Vintage Books.

Meyer, Stephanie. (2005). *Twilight*. Little, Brown and Company.

Meyer, Stephanie. (2006). *New Moon*. Little, Brown and Company.

Meyer, Stephanie. (2007). *Eclipse*. Little, Brown and Company.

Meyer, Stephanie. (2008). *Breaking Dawn*. Little, Brown and Company.

Morrison, Ewan. (August 13, 2012). In the Beginning, There was Fan Fiction: From the Four Gospels to Fifty Shades. *The Guardian*. www.theguardian.com/books/2012/aug/13/fan-fiction-fifty-shades-grey

Slade, David (Director). (2010). *The Twilight Saga: Eclipse* [Film] USA: Summit Entertainment.

Weitz, Chris (Director). (2009). *The Twilight Saga: New Moon* [Film] USA: Summit Entertainment.

Reader Agency as Philosophy

Consumers of *Fifty Shades of Grey* (Taylor-Johnson 2015) actively practice philosophy. They decipher significance from innumerable details making up the film and negotiate many possible lines of logic. They evaluate which stories, ideas, and theories they find feasible or desirable from those they find illogical or ridiculous. They accept some and reject others, while they miss further possible trajectories of thought. They create meaning as they watch and leave the cinema with new or refreshed perspectives about love, sex, gender, power, and law (amongst so many other things). In my next two chapters, I demonstrate the presence of at least two legal interpretations of *Fifty Shades* by analysing *the Scene* through two feminist jurisprudential critiques. In my third reading of *the Scene*, I argue that consumer-bodies are involved in theorising legal concepts while watching movies. This chapter provides a foundation for both by determining that *Fifty Shades* consumers are agents in the philosophical production of cinematic meaning. This is necessary because, as I demonstrate, much of *Fifty Shades* criticism assumes consumers of "women's fiction" are vulnerable to the texts they consume, passively absorbing dangerous ideology. In contrast, feminist scholarship shows that consumers of women's fiction exercise considerable agency. They read and watch with complex engagement, using often maligned texts for validation and exploration as well as indulging in gratifying critique. Watching *Fifty Shades* involves philosophical agency performed by its consumers.

As texts that speak of women's experiences, "women's fiction" involves themes of sex and sexual violence, intimate relationships and intimate partner violence, marriage, property, inheritance, poverty, exploitation, and discrimination, to name a few. Law resides in each of these: demarcating legitimate sex from sexual harm; romance from stalking, assault, and abuse; structuring marriage with rights and obligations; shaping women's capacity to own or inherit; formulating categories of sex; and potentially protecting (but often failing) workers. Even, and perhaps most especially, law resides in those moments when it is not used explicitly to denounce or prevent specific acts. Its absence in fictional instances can implicitly render acts apparently acceptable, thereby potentially influencing audience understandings of

DOI: 10.4324/9780429330414-4

law and justice. Sometimes law's absence is discernible in discomfort, shock or anger when consuming fiction. The implicit residual absence/presence of law means that when we consume popular culture (enjoying, scoffing, weeping, raging) – when we are feeling at once empowered and appalled by *the Scene* – we are responding to and negotiating legal concepts: we are practising jurisprudence.

The Much-Maligned Feminine Text and Consumer

Much of the harsh criticism of *Fifty Shades* expresses concern for women as victims of intimate partner violence. This is due to persistently high rates of gender-based violence and the explicit violence central to the *Fifty Shades* plot. However, the criticism perpetrates similar gender-based violence by denying the agency of millions of women consumers, infantilising them, and blaming them for their ostensible victimhood. *Fifty Shades* consumers are also used as evidence of the texts' deficits; their bodies are simultaneously configured as vulnerable to, and proof of, the texts' dangerousness. This is part of an established culture of condemning women as too embodied to exercise reason. Expressed within academia and across popular media, these criticisms are antithetical to my argument about embodied legal philosophy. However, addressing them helps demonstrate the labour of consumers.

Apprehension about violence against women forms a prominent theme in feminist criticism of *Fifty Shades*. The central romance is identified as gender-based violence. For example, crime writer Casey (2012) describes Christian as bearing "the attributes of so many men . . . who abuse and sometimes end up murdering their intimate partners." Tripodi (2017) states in a sociology journal: "the relationship portrayed . . . is akin to intimate partner violence." Another sociologist, writing for *The Guardian*, describes Christian as a "sexual sociopath who targets . . . an emotionally and sexually unsophisticated 21-year-old" (Dines 2013). With psychologist colleagues, Bonomi et al. (2013, 2014) demonstrates that Christian's behaviours constitute intimate partner violence as defined by the *US Centre for Disease and Prevention Manual*. The depicted violence *is* noteworthy. It replicates many behaviours recognised as violence. Additionally, the way the violence is presented as romance is troubling. Narratives of violence as romance saturate our culture (Johnson and Johnson 2021; Philips 2016). Acute examples include parallels observed between poetry, political philosophy, romantic fiction, subplots in popular movies and scenarios delivered in rape trials to counter complaints of sexual violence (Young 1998; Philadelphoff-Puren 2005; Larcombe 2005; Naffine 1994; Kaspiew 1995–6). These parallels are indicative of broad social acceptance of violence as romance.

However, feminist criticism of *Fifty Shades* expresses concern in ways that cast women consumers as passive victims of the text. The worry for Bonomi et al. (2013) is that women readers internalise these narratives, normalise gendered violence, accept it as part of heterosexuality, interpret controlling behaviour as romantic, and seek violence as proof of love. In *Huffington Post*, Purcell (2013) asserts she is "deeply afraid" for *Fifty Shades* readers. Other feminist commentators censure the franchise as "dangerous" and "damaging" for women (Whitehead 2013; Thorpe 2012). Although these critics are women, they distinguish themselves from women fiction consumers through codes obliquely signifying class. They presume a readership of uncritical victims while excluding themselves from the demographic.

Their concern is regularly delivered with a critique of literary merit implicating and ultimately condemning consumers. Literary critics have consistently labelled women's fiction "low culture," describing it as "feeble and tiresome," "silly," "froth," and "garbage" (Smith 2007, 4). While the assessed merits of a text implicitly judge its consumers, some articulations of a text's value are expressed by directly maligning consumers. Thorpe (2012) describes *Fifty Shades* readers as "average" in her condemnation of the trilogy as lacking "literary merit," while simultaneously worrying about those readers' susceptibility to its romance. Denigration of women consumers is most apparent in the mock genre categorisation of *Fifty Shades* as "mommy porn" (Whitehead 2013). This "cruel and disparaging" nomenclature condemns the texts by ridiculing their consumers (Dymock 2013, 883), casting them as "undiscerning [consumers] of trash" (Harman and Jones 2013, 961). Identified according to their parenting and ingestion of pornography (as opposed to any other aspect of their complex being), these consumers are represented as unsophisticated and self-subjugating, failing to *lean in* to professional life and realise "proper" feminist goals.

Interwoven concern and condemnation reverberate around certain genres – often those that explicitly provoke bodily responses. Williams (1991) calls them "body genres." They are "low" culture. They include action, horror, pornography, and women's fiction as melodrama and romance. As both romance and pornography, *Fifty Shades* is "body genre." In the last two chapters, I explore the film's sensational affects as pornographic romance. Here I note the configuration of bodies in criticisms that simultaneously denounce certain texts for stimulating bodies and infantilise particular consumers as vulnerable to such bodily stimulation. Body genres are condemned as aesthetically deficient due to their lack of subtlety stirring consumer reaction (Williams 1991). This also renders them potentially dangerous. Not all consumers are considered vulnerable. But while "women, blacks, the poor and the elderly" are assumed to be generally "vulnerable" to screen culture (Ang 1985), boys and young men are apparently suspectable to representations of violence such that they may copy what they see (Young 2009; Boyle 2005). Melodrama and romance allegedly indoctrinate women into accepting patriarchal violence (Kapurch 2016). Each vulnerable consumer category resides in binary opposition to educated critics, who are ostensibly able to resist stimulation through the exercise of reason.

The very emergence of women's literacy was accompanied by concerns about female susceptibility to potentially dangerous content (Kapurch 2016). Television is also marked by worry about women consumers' indoctrination (Ang 1985). Accusations of "hysteria" and "feverish" consumption bespeak critics' understandings of women as vulnerable to the sensations of their bodies, unable to exercise rational thought, and thus susceptible to the influence of explicitly stimulating texts (Kapurch 2016, 9). Women's unruly bodies and associated lack of reason are echoed in *the Scene*. In my *Third Reading: Legal Sensations* I analyse Christian's negation of Ana's refusal to sex by reading "the truth" of her consent in signs of her body's arousal. Christian's assumption that he can read Ana's body better than she can is shared by law's denial of women's assertions of agency, repeatedly reading the truth of their desires (and consent to sex) in their bodies (Young 1998). Women are imagined as unable to control their bodies, nor to know them. Further, they are apparently at the mercy of their bodies as consumers and sexual beings.

Ultimately, *Fifty Shades* consumers are simultaneously worried about and presented as proof that the texts are bad. These consumers are imagined as not educated, feminist, or critically engaged enough to know better. I oppose this by arguing that consumers of women's fiction are active and agentic: they negotiate ideas and generate meaning. Thus, rather than passively ingesting violence as romance, consumers of texts like *Fifty Shades* often feel validated in recognising their own experiences represented, exercising their own pleasurable critique, and finding opportunities for resisting dominant discourses. Such engagement is potentially made possible because the text itself appears conservative and hegemonically unthreatening. Not only are these complex engagements with text, they also involve philosophical grappling with theories of gender, sex, and law.

Hidden in Plain Sight

Ziv (1994, 73) suggests it is naïve to expect a piece of fiction to radically subvert convention because it is female-authored. Authors "cannot simply extricate" their texts from dominant discourse (73). Hegemonic power works through our language, grammar, and metaphor, shaping our logic and even the way that we see (Berger 1972). To flout established patterns of signification risks incomprehensibility – alienating potential publishers, producers, and audiences. However, subversive potential exists within ostensibly conservative products. Nonconforming ideas, narratives, and intensities of feeling can shimmer tantalisingly to be momentarily grasped by consumers with relevant cultural training. Feminist cultural analysts have found resistance and empowerment for consumers in women's fiction, and validation of particularly gendered experiences of heterosexuality that are often unseen, ignored or denied in broader culture. *Fifty Shades* contains potentially subversive content hidden in plain sight between episodes of patriarchal heteronormative pornographic romance.

Contemporary women's fiction as "chick lit," is an exemplifying site of resistance and empowering negotiations of culturally political contexts. Ugandan and South African chick lit, for example, interrogates the realities of women's lives "concerning love, marriage and motherhood . . . intimacy and desire" in ways that offer "new feminine subjectivities" within contexts of uncertainty and political unrest (Spencer 2018, 155). Meanwhile, British Muslim chick lit offers "new articulations of Muslim womanhood that question the terms of neoliberal consumer-driven gender regimes as well as those dictated by traditional cultural mores" (Newns 2018, 286). This women's fiction critiques dominant discourses, allowing consumers to forge nonconforming understandings about themselves and their worlds.

Despite *Fifty Shades'* contrastingly white heteronormativity, Dymock (2013, 881–882) identifies a "promise [of] something relatively taboo . . . concealed within a conservative form." Access to "previously off-limits sexual fantasy" is made possible for many women because it is offered within otherwise non-threateningly heteronormative material (882). The combination of "familiar romance tropes of emotional intimacy with graphic scenes of 'kinky' sex, which appear to defy standard conceptions of 'feminine' sexual interests," helps readers to "thwart common cultural expectations and to supply gratification ordinarily ruled out by the way . . . culture structures their lives" (Deller and Smith 2013, 947). Analysis of online forum discussions appears to confirm this by observing the use of *Fifty Shades* to discuss sex, sexuality, and relationships (Jones and Mills 2014). Notably, such forums include religiously conservative women (Whitehead 2013). The conventional packaging of *Fifty Shades* enables some women consumers access to sexual fantasies and identities they are usually denied.

For some women, being seen reading these books is "to engage in a public debate about female sexuality" (Deller and Smith 2013, 937). This echoes the 1970s housewives Radway (1984) interviewed, who used their romance reading as a tool to resist the unrelenting demands of domesticity, even if only momentarily. In both instances, resistance and subversion work through the discursive instruments available. For Radway's women, reading a book quietly enabled women to create boundaries and not attend to their children or husbands for a brief period. For Deller and Smith's women, it means quietly asserting the legitimacy of female sexual desire in public spaces. Both are acts of political engagement tempered by ostensibly unthreatening romance.

Women's fiction can also be a source of validation. Rather than indoctrinating consumers into accepting violence as romance, scholarship indicates that women's fiction provides gratification by reflecting consumers' lived experiences, including its depictions of *romance as violence* (Ziv 1994). The extravagance of the genre's sensation and emotion offers further validation when hegemonic culture diminishes, denies, and justifies men's violence against women. Women's experiences and emotions are taken seriously in women's fiction, as marked by the drama. It is the critics who do not when they disparage the texts.

Fifty Shades is controversial because it presents violence recognisable as pervasive throughout heterosexuality. This is a lived reality for many heterosexual women. Rather than being presented as unproblematically romantic within *Fifty Shades*, the violence is flagged as troubling. Ana's "feminine" uncertainty concerns Christian's violence. While she is depicted as attracted to him, her discomfort with the way he expresses his desire and performs intimacy is central to the texts. Christian's stalking and controlling behaviours are marked as simultaneously romantic and disturbing to Ana. A key example is the final sex act. In this sequence, Ana has asked Christian to show her "how much it can hurt." By "it" she means his desired BDSM practice. As the cinematic version moves towards him striking her bottom with his belt, her active consent is underscored by Christian's script: "We're here because you said yes." Immediately following the agreed-upon sixth strike, she is repulsed: she "wants none of him" (James 2012, 506). What ensues in the book is six pages of internalised dilemma:

> *What was I thinking?* . . . He warned me . . . He won't want to be with me if I can't give him this . . . the thought of not seeing him again practically chokes me . . . I asked for it . . . The thought lies heavy . . . He has never made love to me, has he? It's always been fucking to him.
>
> (506–512)

Ana does not want the sex Christian does. Neither does she want his lavish gifts or control. Yet she wants him and *some kind* of sexual intimacy, even what she calls "kinky-fuckery." Ana expresses discomfort, unease, and anger about Christian's violence, moments of ambiguously non-consensual sex, and even sex acts she has consented to but is troubled by. The complete *Fifty Shades* trilogy depicts a young woman navigating a path through heteronormative structures and rape culture to negotiate interesting sex she enjoys but does not hurt her in ways she does not want.

Sexual and intimate partner violence remains a pervasive threat for women resembling Ana. Throughout the world, it is estimated that one in three women experience intimate partner violence and/or sexual violence (www.who.int). Most of this violence is perpetrated by current or former male intimate partners (www.unwomen.org). In Australia, more than one woman a week is killed by current or former intimate male partners, while one in five women report experiencing some form of sexual violence since reaching 15 years of age (www.ourwatch.org.au/quickfacts/).

The unease about romance shared by heterosexual women and Ana also concerns the difficulty of identifying which men are dangerous. Gottzén and

Berggren (2021, 77) demonstrate masculinity as something that is not stable nor consistent but "always contradictory and contingent." They argue that "inclusive" masculinities – supportive of feminist ideals – can be performed simultaneously with " 'orthodox' masculinity that is . . . sexist and violent" (77). The same man can inhabit both dissonant masculinities. When ostensibly feminist men can harbour the potential for intimate partner violence, the dangers presented by masculinity can be experienced as a pervasive fear or discomfort for heterosexual women. How can you distinguish which man is safe and not harbouring some form of toxic masculinity? Such discomfort is expressed in texts like *Fifty Shades*.

The pervasive threat of hetero-masculine violence is recognisable in other women's fiction as reflecting consumers' life concerns. For example, although the television series about a teenager protecting society from demons presents an empowering role model for young women, *Buffy the Vampire Slayer* (Wheedon 1997–2003) also sustains a persistent motif that "sex is dangerous for women" (Siegal 2007, 82). The series thrives on romantic tension driven by Buffy's attraction to a sequence of male characters. But for Buffy, sex "always involves power imbalances and emotional, if not physical, violence" (82). Consequently, the heroine repeatedly renounces her desires. Siegal (75) states that this depiction of heterosexuality "strongly" reflects dilemmas faced by young women "within . . . mainstream culture." The series taps into an experience of heterosexual womanhood familiar to its consumers.

Correspondingly, in *Twilight* (Meyer 2005) the struggles of the female lead mirror those of its consumers. While *Twilight* depicts a similarly fraught relationship to that in *Fifty Shades*, the gendered issues navigated by the heroine extend to broader cultural conditions of femininity. Kapurch (2016, 5) found that teenaged girls identified powerfully with its representation of the "paralysing effects of self-consciousness brought on by social judgement and restrictions related to gender, class and age." This representation corresponds strongly with the "actual controls associated with the social construction of . . . twenty-first-century girlhood" (5). Kapurch's readers thus felt both empathy and empowerment through recognition of their own emotional struggles and feelings of powerlessness in *Twilight*.

For Ziv (1994, 67), women's recognition of their own experience in fiction potentially exposes "hidden assumptions of patriarchal ideology." Their discomfort, frustration, or anger about the conditions of their lives are confirmed when represented in fiction. Women's fiction supports consumers to see the causes of their feelings and discern the structures of patriarchy. Thus, rather than viewing women's fiction as modelling or romanticising victimised femininity, we might understand consumers gaining strength and validation from such depictions.

Meanwhile, the hyperbolic aesthetic of melodrama authenticates emotions experienced by consumers outside the text (Kapurch 2016). Radway's (1984, 70) romance readers identify "completely with the wronged heroine and vicariously participate in her shock and outrage" as their books depict heteronormalised violence. Meanwhile, melodramatic storylines in soap operas "function as metaphors for" the torments of life beyond the screen (Ang 1985). By provoking emotional reactions through the identification of shared experience, consuming women's fiction works like "a kind of release valve for pent-up anger and resentment" that many consumers cannot express "in the context of their own worlds" (Radway 1984, 70). Thus, through their apparent *melodramatic* exaggeration, these texts provide sites of recognition and shared dissatisfaction with the structural limitations throughout consumers' lived experiences. Further than this, women's fiction provides safe spaces in which consumers may *feel* and *express* emotions the external world will not tolerate.

The considerable failure of dominant culture to acknowledge women's experiences of violence is repeated in Christian's attempt to overwrite Ana's refusal to sex in *the Scene*. While this echoes rape law's reading consent in women's bodies against their articulated non-consent, it is also shared by such hegemonic institutions as psychology, medicine, philosophy, education, politics, literature, and art. Each of these disciplines has dismissed, pathologised, ridiculed, and criminalised expressions of women's experience. Feminist criticism of *Fifty Shades* replicates the silencing pattern by expressing concern for women consumers' vulnerability to representations of gendered violence while also deriding them for their choice of fiction.

In contrast, women's fiction can provide spaces where women's experiences, knowledges, and feelings can be articulated, shared, recognised, and validated. The hyperbolic emotion depicted in and generated by women's fiction plays a part in the gratification of their consumption. Further than this, the intensities of feeling are meaningful to women consumers in ways that defy hegemonic discourses – discourses which cannot and will not accurately capture, comprehend, or articulate so much of the women's experience. In my last chapter, I explore embodied resonances of women's fiction (with a focus on *the Scene*) for the ways in which they entangle audience bodies in the text and shape the ideas and theories that consumers generate *in concert with* each text. However, next, I demonstrate the labour exercised by consumers of women's fiction.

Pleasure in Critique

While critics of *Fifty Shades* implicitly separate consumers as either erudite or crude, feminist culture theorists argue that differently positioned consumers use a range of techniques to make sense of and enjoy popular culture. Correlating reading practices with patriarchal power structures, Brown (1994) divides readers into masculine and feminine categories. But correspondent with the multifarious ways through which power works, as well as diversity and intersectionality beyond the gender binary, there are many and varied strategies used by consumers to interpret their texts. In this book, I predominantly focus on women consumers of women's fiction as the category most strongly associated with *Fifty Shades*, demonstrating that this group is far from homogenous and that multiple interpretations of a text can be generated, simultaneously, even by a single consumer. Further than this, feminist scholarship suggests that there is considerable pleasure in the labour of active reading, including criticism (or "hate reading").

For Brown (1994), to be a *masculine* reader is to be affiliated with the hegemonic order: your experience and knowledge are reinforced by, and reinforces, dominant logic and conventions. Heteronormativity is also a powerful lens such that where a character's sexuality is not indicated, hegemonic reading practices "dictates that heterosexuality can be assumed while homosexuality must be proved" (Jones cited by Tosenberger 2008, 202). Thus, although "the queerness of texts is pervasive" it is "not obvious to heterocentrist straights" (Doty 1993, xiii). It is "too subtle for readers lacking queer consciousness" (Tosenberger 2008, 202). A privilege of heterosexual, masculine consumers is that they do not have to recognise the stories or logics that do not align with their own. Their experiences and knowledges are justified as they align with prevailing philosophy, whilst ignoring, dismissing, pathologising, ridiculing, criminalising . . . those who diverge.

Meanwhile, marginalised and resistant consumers are often literate on multiple discursive planes. Out of necessity, they must navigate dominant discourses. However, differently diverging consumers may have varying degrees of proficiency in discourses articulating assorted subjugated experiences and knowledges. Due to the *angle of their arrival*, a consumer may be alert to various *shimmers* fleetingly signifying otherwise hidden ideas and narratives. Each consumer's singular cultural training, their acculturated sensorium, is informed by the communities of which they are a part or with which they are allied. Various communities of women recognise shared experiences – as in women's fiction – that focus on the details of women's intimate lives, the worries that plague female heterosexuality, and the dangers of male violence against women. There are also intensities of feeling triggered by shimmering subjugated significances in a conservative or counter text that might be shared by communities of consumers, but not registered by masculine consumers or accepted by the hegemonic order.

Juxtaposing the female subjectivity of concerned feminist critics against that of the presumed *Fifty Shades* audience illustrates how schools of interpretative practice are not simply divided according to binary gender categories. In this instance, class and education also shape the way consumers approach the text. Race, sexuality, neurodiversity and ableness are further intersections of subjecthood texturing readings of *Fifty Shades*. Thus, while different women nimbly navigate numerous masculine fields of discourse and wield the interpretive tools of privilege to assess the hierarchical worth of cultural products as educated, middle-class scholars and critics, there are many discursive threads they each varyingly may not perceive.

I argue that many women consume individual texts from multiple perspectives simultaneously. Sometimes despite their political allegiances. As Ang (1985, 92) observes, enjoyment of a text "does not preclude a political or moral condemnation of its production context or its ideological content." My friends and I relished *Twilight* as an enjoyment of conventional romance and through pleasures in critique – all while recognising shimmers of validation, empowerment and dissent in the films. Consumers of *Fifty Shades* are literate across many discursive planes that *masculine* readers are not because *masculine* readers do not need to be, and perhaps do not want to be.

The dexterity of women consumers extends beyond decoding signs. They critically engage with form and practice flexible, active identification with multiple aspects of the texts they enjoy. Through interviews with teenaged girls, Blackford (2004, 5) found they "have sophisticated ways of engaging with literature." They use their knowledge of storytelling traditions and are attentive to narrative strategy. Kapurch's (2016, 18) girl-readers engage "on an aesthetic level." In both studies, girl readers did not "singularly identify" with specific characters based on shared subjectivity such as gender, age, or ethnicity but worked to "imagine other characters' points of view" (Kapurch 2016, 18). Instead of being bound through identification to one character, their presence within each text was regularly "as an omniscient gaze" (Blackford 2004, 19). These readers actively shifted perspective, from external consideration of style, narrative and technique, through to multiple identification with diverse characters. Feminist research demonstrates that women's reading practices are far from passive and susceptible: they are active, perceptive, and erudite.

The skills and activity of teenaged girls contrast the formative theory of cinematic identification. Mulvey (2006) argues that cinema coerces audiences to identify with male characters. Consequently, women are compelled to "cross-identify" – across the ostensible gender binary. Steinbock (2019) argues that far more cross-identification happens in cinema than this. In my third reading of *the Scene*, I explore the corporeality of deep empathic (embodied) identification. Here I note that while techniques of narrative, authorship, cinematography, and so on, encourage identification along certain lines, many consumers actively identify across identity categories regularly and with pleasure.

The sophistication with which so many consumers engage with women's fiction is evident in their critical conversations. Critique is an important element of women's consuming practices. Consumers of women's fiction pick and choose their preferred texts and critically evaluate what they read. Like my friends and I watching *Twilight*, these women often love to hate what they consume. This can involve "reactive pleasures" – the rebellious enjoyment of recognising when your politics do not align with the hegemony (Brown 1994, 18). Critical conversations with like-minded consumers regularly enhance the gratification of consumption. These conversations evidence the substantive quality of consumer philosophy exercised during the leisurely digestion of popular culture.

Since Radway's (1984) work with romance readers, scholarship has documented the critical agency of women consumers. For example, Radway's readers select their books according to exacting narrative preferences (a professional heroine +/- a rude but devoted hero +/- multiple rape scenarios, and so on). Brown's (1994) soap opera viewers analyse each episode, assessing the way women are portrayed, while many of Ang's (1985) *Dallas* fans enjoy mocking the series and watch with irony. More recently, Rowntree (2015, 521) finds chick lit consumers "clearly critical"; enjoying representations of female sexual agency but desiring "more diverse and alternative portrayals of women's sexuality." Meanwhile, Kapurch (2016, 7) observes young *Twilight* fans evaluating depictions of masculinity and debating male characters as models for romantic partners. In each instance, consumers are exercising critique while enjoying women's fiction.

Fan cultures provide further evidence of critical engagement. For example, *Fifty Shades* was created as *Twilight* fanfiction. "Correction" of original texts is common, demonstrating evaluation and reflection rather than indoctrination of consumers. Queer fandom as a "lively, stimulating and tolerant interpretative community" is energised by critical analysis of narrative credibility, character motivation and behaviour (Tosenberger 2008, 202). It can also be a "political battlefield" in which consumers insist "on the primacy of their own interpretations," above and beyond the author's voice (Duggan 2022, 148). Dyer (2021) calls fandom a "critical pedagogy," in which consumers generate pleasure together through analysing shared texts. Tosenberger's (2008) analysis of Harry Potter fandom reveals a level of enjoyment in critically and productively engaging with texts that is akin to orgasmic *jouissance* in terms of being beyond existent discursive expression. While fan culture can be explicit in its productivity and diversity, it suggests that similar active pleasures might be practiced in more inconspicuous ways by consumers of women's fiction.

Fifty Shades fans are critical and analytical. While fan sites and online discussion forums include mocking critiques (Deller and Smith 2013), when interviewed, other consumers identified elements of the texts they found unappealing (Bonomi et al. 2013). These interviewees generated "a consistently robust narrative" about the central relationship being "unhealthy, dangerous and harmful" (142). They recognised a correlation between the extreme value of Christian's gifts and intensification in his "desire to control" Ana (142). While these consumers felt the thrill of the gifts, they also expressed critical awareness of the gendered power dynamics of which the gifts are a part. Their enjoyment of the text did not blind them to the patriarchal violence contained within.

Harman and Jones (2013, 952) suggest *Fifty Shades* has "generated an ironic, even guilty, fandom in which readers and viewers bemoan the series' flaws, while enjoying (sometimes furtively) the texts." These fans, they argue, include academic and media critics who have consumed *Fifty Shades* as the "hated text *par excellence*," relishing the pleasures of deploring a text (952). This echoes Ang's (1985) *Dallas* watchers, who consumed a television series they found morally and politically problematic with irony and mockery. Through this lens, the "vulnerable" consumers of *Fifty Shades* are potentially a "constructed Other . . . an imagined spectre" (anonymous in Deller and Smith 2013, 961). Their pleasure in the texts might actually involve exercising vital agency in *hate-reading* or reading *Fifty Shades* critically (Harman and Jones 2013).

Mocking critique, critical forum discussions and hate-reading resemble *reactive pleasures* or enjoyment derived from "understanding that one's ideological positioning is problematic in our culture" (Brown 1994, 18). Reactive pleasures can be more gratifying when they are shared. Critical conversations about texts generate "much of the meaning" associated with the original texts (Brown 1994, 12–13). Designating such conversations "tertiary texts," thereby granting them the status of "text," culture theorists disrupt the hierarchies of low and high culture implicit in criticisms of *Fifty Shades* (Brown 1994, 12–13). It also acknowledges the substantive quality of these conversations as meaningful and bearing potentially material implications. Such implications include forum discussions in which women use *Fifty Shades* to talk about their own sex lives (Whitehead 2013) and the increase in sex toy sales (Jones and Mills 2014, 241). Consuming *Fifty Shades* has potentially supported a range of women to explore new forms of sexual play. Consumers of women's fiction create meaningful texts and materialise their interpretations beyond the product created by authors, directors, cinematographers, and so on.

Contrary to feminist critics, consumers of women's fiction exert complex reading practices, out of necessity and for pleasure. They engage with their chosen texts at multiple levels, evaluate the content, interpret different layers of signification, identify with numerous characters simultaneously, and read both the minute detail and larger narrative structures with an awareness of convention, technique and aesthetic mores. They mock, resist and mobilise texts to comprehend and negotiate social structures that often bind them. They are highly skilled in their practice. Consuming women's fiction involves agency and activity.

These practices are philosophical: they interpret the world, generate logic, and construct meaning. And while philosophers might only interpret the world, these consumers change it because they implement their philosophy, using it to think and do the rest of their everyday lives.

Reader Agency as Jurisprudence

During *the Scene* in *Fifty Shades of Grey*, consumers are philosophically engaged with ideas about law. The theories at play concern the power of contracts as means to navigate sexual intimacy; what constitutes consent; the legitimacy of sex with/out consent; what can/not be consensual. When critical engagements with cinema touch on the legal concepts presented within their text, consumers are renegotiating their legal knowledge. This knowledge then informs their navigation of the world beyond the cinema, including their knowledge of law. Even when watching the most maligned of women's fiction in our leisure time (when our "critical thinking" is ostensibly switched off), we are busily playing with legal ideas and generating new interpretations which we may well implement in future interactions with the social world. I go on to argue that we are doing this in and through our bodies. We then use our embodied legal philosophy when engaging in legal practices, like performing jury duty or having sex – potentially rendering even our sex jurisprudential.

The next step in my argument is to provide a brief description of *the Scene* before delivering two possible feminist legal interpretations of it. Then in my third reading, I demonstrate how our bodies are engaged by *the Scene* to evidence that our beating hearts, twitching fingers, and flushing genitalia are all part of jurisprudential practice.

Bibliography

Ang, Ien. (1985). *Watching Dallas: Soap Opera and the Melodramatic Imagination*. Taylor and Franci.

Berger, John. (1972). *Ways of Seeing*. Penguin.

Blackford, Holly Virginia. (2004). *Out of This World: Why Literature Matters to Girls*. Teachers College Press.

Bonomi, Amy E., Altenburger, Lauren E., and Walton, Nicole L. (2013). "Double Crap!" Abuse and Harmed Identity in *Fifty Shades of Grey*. *Journal of Women's Health*, 22(9), pp. 733–744.

Bonomi, Amy E., Nemeth, Julianna M., Altenburger, Lauren E., Anderson, Melissa L., Snyder, Anastasia, and Dotto, Irma. (2014). Fiction or Not? *Fifty Shades* is Associated with Health Risks in Adolescent and Young Adult Females. *Journal of Women's Health*, 23(9), pp. 720–728.

Boyle, Karen. (2005). *Media and Violence: Gendering the Debates*. Sage Publications.

Brown, Mary Ellen. (1994). *Soap Opera and Women's Talk: The Pleasure of Resistance*. Sage.

Casey, Kathryn. (June 23, 2012). Is 'Fifty Shades of Grey' Dangerous? *Forbes*. www.forbes.com/sites/crime/2012/06/23/is-fifty-shades-of-grey-dangerous/?sh=43756053466e

Deller, Ruth A., and Smith, Clarissa. (2013). Reading the BDSM Romance: Reader Responses to *Fifty Shades*. *Sexualities*, 16(8), pp. 932–950.

Dines, Gail. (October 26, 2013). Don't be Fooled by Fifty Shades of Grey – Christian Grey is No Heartthrob. *The Guardian*. www.theguardian.com/commentisfree/2013/oct/25/fifty-shades-of-grey-christian-jamie-dornan-fall

Doty, Alexander. (1993). Whose Text is It Anyway?: Queer Cultures, Queer Auteurs, and Queer Authorship. *Quarterly Review of Film & Video*, 15(1), pp. 41–54.
Duggan, Jennifer. (2022). Transformative Readings: Harry Potter Fan Fiction, Trans/Queer Reader Response, and J. K. Rowling. *Children's Literature in Education*, 53, pp. 147–168.
Dyer, Connor. (2021). Critical Pedagogy and Visual Culture Art Education in a Cosplay-Based Curriculum. *Transformative Works and Cultures*, 35, no pagination.
Dymock, Alex. (2013). Flogging Sexual Transgression: Interrogating the Costs of the '*Fifty Shades* Effect'. *Sexualities*, 16(8), pp. 880–895.
Gottzén, Lucas, and Berggren, Kalle. (2021). The Rape Capital or the Most Gender-Equal Country in the World? Masculinity, Hybridity and Young Men's Intimate Partner Violence in Sweden. In Gottzén, Lucas, Bjørnholt, Margunn, and Boonzaier, Floretta (Eds). *Men, Masculinities and Intimate Partner Violence* (pp. 66–80). Routledge.
Harman, Sarah, and Jones, Bethan. (2013). Fifty Shades of Ghey: Snark Fandom and the Figure of the Anti-Fan. *Sexualities*, 16(8), pp. 951–968.
James, E. L. (2012). *Fifty Shades of Grey*. Vintage Books.
Johnson, Nicole L., and Johnson, Dawn M. (2021). An Empirical Exploration into the Measurement of Rape Culture. *Journal of Interpersonal Violence*, 36(1–2), pp. 70–95.
Jones, Lucy, and Mills, Sara. (2014). Analysing Agency: Reader Responses to *Fifty Shades of Grey*. *Gender and Language*, 8(2), pp. 225–244.
Kapurch, Katie. (2016). *Victorian Melodrama in the Twenty-First Century*. Palgrave.
Kaspiew, Rae. (1995–6). Rape Lore: Legal Narratives and Sexual Violence. *Melbourne University Law Review*, 20, pp. 350–382.
Larcombe, Wendy. (2005). *Compelling Engagements: Feminism,* Rape Law and Romance Fiction. The Federation Press.
Meyer, Stephanie. (2005). *Twilight*. Little, Brown and Company.
Mulvey, Laura. (2006). Visual Pleasure and Narrative Cinema. In Merck, Mandy (Ed). *The Sexual Subject: Screen Reader in Sexuality* (pp. 22–34). Routledge.
Naffine, Ngaire. (1994). Possession: Erotic Law and the Law of Rape. *Modern Law Review*, 57, pp. 10–37.
Newns, Lucinda. (2018). Renegotiating Romantic Genres: Textual Resistance and Muslim Chick Lit. *Journal of Commonwealth Literature*, 53(2), pp. 284–300.
Philadelphoff-Puren, Nina. (2005). Contextualising Consent: The Problem of Rape and Romance. *Australian Feminist Studies*, 20(46), pp. 31–42.
Philips, Nickie. (2016). *Beyond Blurred Lines: Rape Culture in Popular Media*. Rowman and Littlefield Publishers.
Purcell, Carey. (March 4, 2013). *Fifty Shades of Feminism – a Response to E. L. James* [Blog Post]. www.careypurcell.com/articles/8141
Radway, Janice A. (1984). *Reading the Romance: Women, Patriarchy, and Popular Literature*. University of North Carolina Press.

Rowntree, Margaret R. (2015). Feminine Sexualities in the Chick Genre. *Feminist Media Studies*, 15(3), pp. 508–521.

Siegel, Carol. (2007). Female Heterosexual Sadism: The Final Feminist Taboo in *Buffy the Vampire Slayer* and the Anita Blake Vampire Hunter Series. In Johnson, Merri Lisa (Ed). *Third Wave Feminism and Television: Jane Puts It in a Box* (pp. 56–90). I. B. Tauris.

Smith, Caroline J. (2007). *Cosmopolitan Culture and Consumerism in Chick Lit*. Routledge.

Spencer, Lynda Gichanda. (2018). "Having It All"?: (Re) Examining Conspicuous Consumption and Pernicious Masculinities in South African Chick-Lit. *English in Africa*, 45(3), pp. 79–97.

Steinbock, Eliza. (2019). *Shimmering Images: Trans Cinema, Embodiment, and the Aesthetics of Change*. Duke University Press.

Taylor-Johnson, Samantha (Director). (2015). *Fifty Shades of Grey* [Film] Focus Features, Michael De Luca Productions, Trigger Street Productions, Universal Pictures.

Thorpe, Vanessa. (July 1, 2012). Why Does Fifty Shades of Grey Turn British Women on? *The Guardian*. www.theguardian.com/books/2012/jun/30/fifty-shades-grey-women-sadomasochism

Tosenberger, Catherine. (2008). Homosexuality at the Online Hogwarts: Harry Potter Slash Fanfiction. *Children's Literature*, 36(1), pp. 185–207.

Tripodi, Francesca. (2017). Fifty Shades of Consent? *Feminist Media Studies*, 17(1), pp. 93–107.

Wheedon, Chris (Director). (1997–2003). *Buffy the Vampire Slayer* [Television] USA: 20th Century Fox Television.

Whitehead, Deborah. (2013). When Religious 'Mommy Bloggers' Met 'Mommy Porn': Evangelical and Mormon Women's Responses to *Fifty Shades*. *Sexualities*, 16(8), pp. 915–931.

Williams, Linda. (1991). Film Bodies: Gender, Genre and Excess. *Film Quarterly*, 44(4), pp. 2–13.

Young, Alison. (1998). The Wasteland of the Law, the Wordless Song of the Rape Victim. *Melbourne University Law Review*, 22(2), pp. 442–465.

Young, Alison. (2009). *The Scene of Violence: Cinema, Crime, Affect*. Routledge.

Ziv, Amalia. (1994). The Pervert's Progress: An Analysis of 'Story of O' and the Beauty Trilogy. *Feminist Review*, 49, pp. 61–75.

Interlude – *The Scene*

In a boardroom, the sounds are sharp and clear as Ana empties her document file – paper brushing against paper and pen hitting tabletop. Music begins as playful violin and xylophone while the camera pans quickly over the document head showing it is a CONTRACT between parties titled "the DOMINANT" and "the SUBMISSIVE." We hear the rattle of Christian's pen as we see him swing it between his fingers.

Ana sighs. A wide shot shows the two silhouetted against orange light, sitting at opposite ends of a table flanked by six chairs.

"Impressive." Ana states.

Christian: "I've done this before."

Cut to Ana looking discomforted. Cut to Christian with a little smile. "Business meetings, I mean."

"Oh, ah," Ana smiles and looks down.

"Miss Steele, your meeting."

After an extreme close-up of Ana taking a deep breath, she asserts loudly "Page one, strike out my old address." The image cuts back to the wide shot of the boardroom and the negotiations begin.

The dialogue mimics legal language, numbering sections and subsections, clarifying terms, naming appendices, striking out soft and hard limits, while "duly noting" others. The pop pseudo-legal language climaxes almost immediately with a quote from the contract:

> The submissive shall submit to any activity demanded by the dominant and shall do so without hesitation or argument.

Tight shots show a pen definitively crossing out words as Ana refuses the use of some sex toys and acts, accepting others. She sets boundaries concerning her body. Ostensibly, she is voluntarily negotiating a contract for the mutual satisfaction of both herself and Christian.

Then there is a moment of dissembling. She becomes the naïve Ana of previous scenes, asking, "What are butt plugs?" At that moment two women, sheathed in tight "corporate" attire and immaculate hair, wordlessly enter the

DOI: 10.4324/9780429330414-5

room delivering food and wine. A hollow "clop" suggests stilettoes on bare floor in the distinct musical pause. Ana is silent until they leave, covering documents on the table, her eyes throwing nervous glances. She regains her composure when they exit, jibing "You must go through many disclosure agreements."

"My staff know only what I choose to tell them . . . Please resume, Miss Steele." The music that returns has an edge of tension.

"Can I just say how impressed I am by your commitment to this meeting?" In this "spirit" Christian offers to "throw in a sweetener." He proposes to include an aspect of heterosexual romance Ana has requested: regular dates. Once a week, "on a day of your choosing" they go out for dinner, a movie, or ice skating. "Just like a regular couple."

"Accepted. You are very kind." A piano emphasises this moment as touchingly romantic.

A tight shot shows Ana winding red tape on the document file, indicating negotiations are over. Again, the sound focuses on stationary: paper against table, a pen rolled between fingers.

The screen cuts to Ana's point of view as Christian drops his pen decisively on the table and declares he wants to "fuck you into the middle of next week."

"You're not fighting fair." She utters quietly.

"I never have."

Pause.

"I will review these changes and try to come to a decision." Ana is in medium shot, looking at the file and playing with her pen.

"You wanna leave?" he asks.

"Yes."

"But your body tells me something different." Christian describes Ana's thighs pressing together, her breathing and the flush of her cheeks as signs of desire. Violins and bass guitar return with the growing sexual tension. Ana prompts Christian to describe the sex that would ensue. He tells her he would "help her out of that little dress." He anticipates finding her naked beneath. He holds his tie taught across his fists.

"Really?" she encourages.

"And then I would bend you over . . ."

"Right here on this table?" Ana stretches her forearm and places her palm on the table. In a close shot, it is a sensual gesture. The audience are encouraged to feel themselves feeling the tabletop, perhaps cool and smooth. Shot and reverse shot show parted lips.

Suddenly, Ana thanks Christian formally for the meeting, and the sound of stilettoes indicates her exit.

Christian is left open-mouthed, staring straight ahead.

First Reading

The *Frisson* of Sexual Agency

In the prelude it appears that Ana has won. She has considered Christian's contract, indulged his sexual fantasy, and resisted both. She has withheld her consent, asserted her authority, and exercised her power. The contract seems to have granted Ana sexual agency, enabling her to determine the boundaries of her bodily integrity.

This is an optimistic liberal feminist interpretation of *the Scene* I analyse from *Fifty Shades of Grey* (Taylor-Johnson 2015). Liberal feminism has had significant impacts upon laws regulating sex and intimate relationships, with rape law reform designed to better represent the experience of sexual violence survivors. Contract and consent are central to liberal feminist reconceptualisations of rape. I trace a liberal feminist jurisprudence in *the Scene* that presents contract and consent as empowering tools for young women navigating sex and intimacy. My purpose is to demonstrate the presence of law in *the Scene*. But also, to show how this presence is *jurisprudential* in terms of offering a specifically identifiable theoretical understanding of how law works. In the next chapter, I present a second feminist interpretation. Together, the readings illustrate that more than one theory of law is available in the text. This allows me to argue that consumers evaluate different legal arguments while they watch – that consumers are theorising law. My focus on sensation and affect in the third reading of *the Scene* then shows how this jurisprudence at the cinema involves consumers' bodies, to argue that consumers are performing embodied legal philosophy at the cinema.

I begin this chapter with a brief explanation of feminist liberal legal theory as it pertains to contract and consent in the context of sex and rape. What follows is divided into an analysis of three liberal concepts signified in *the Scene*: equality, autonomy, and neutrality. I trace these pillars of feminist liberal philosophy in the characterisation of *the Scene's* contract, *mise-en-scène*, and costuming, and show how they support an optimistic understanding of contract and consent as empowering for women negotiating heterosexual intimacy.

DOI: 10.4324/9780429330414-6

Rape and Feminist Liberal Philosophy

The contract is the most obvious manifestation of law in *the Scene*. However, law also exists in most contemporary conceptualisations of sex due to law's role in distinguishing "legitimate" from "criminal" sexual contact. Most particularly, law haunts representations of sex as the perceived absence or presence of consent. Consent is a unit of law that circulates throughout culture, giving texture to our dreams and performances of sex. We are often presented with contracts and consent as simple tools we can implement to support our interactions with others and protect ourselves from harm. These tools also promise us the autonomy to undertake painful or potentially "risky" activities such as body modification, BDSM, medical procedures, dangerous sports and more. However, rather than being universally self-evident concepts, the significance of contract and consent is rooted in a specific cultural history. A contract forms liberalism's origin story for contemporary Western democratic societies. The social contract is a transformative tale in which people agree to give up their freedoms (in a state of nature) and obey law in exchange for protections and benefits offered by a sovereign (monarch or parliament). The agreement establishes society. Due to the centrality of the contract, the story lends meaning to other instances of contract and informs feminist liberalism's rape law reform. The philosophy of the social contract accessible within *the Scene* as legal theory potentially shapes the meanings consumers generate as they watch.

Contemporary rape law is informed by social contract ideology, which encodes sexual encounters with philosophically liberal significance (Munro 2008, 923–924). Cowan (2007, 92) states that consent is "philosophically and practically, the focal point of sexual assault." As such, consent is the marker distinguishing legitimate from illegitimate sexual activity, operating as the transformative core differentiating between "harmful" and "harmless," with "rape" defined in terms of absent consent (Munro 2008, 924). Many criminal jurisdictions now reinforce this classification by legislating definitions of consent as "free agreement" or "free and voluntary" (Douglas 2008, 109). In Victorian law (Australia), for example, such qualification reinforces the idea that consent is not present when a person is asleep or unconscious, and that consent cannot be coerced. Pateman (1988) argues that "contract is . . . the paradigm of free agreement." Through the lens of consent as free agreement, sexual intimacy is configured as contractual. Sexual encounters are reconceptualised as ongoing contractual conversations in a "communicative model of consent" (Douglas 2008; Powell et al. 2013). The centrality of consent to sexual offence law, and particularly rape law, shapes the ways in which we imagine, perform and experience sex. Contract lies at the heart of contemporary sexual intimacy.

Throughout jurisprudential and political philosophy of contract, numerous contract types are rendered analogous and used to comprehend and justify each other. Accordingly, Cott (2002) traces the metaphorical use of marriage contracts to explain and legitimise a particular structure of government during the foundation of the United States of America. Similarly, Pateman (1988) demonstrates the ways in which formal and informal slave, employment, marriage, and sex contracts have all been used by social contract theorists since the seventeenth century to imagine how the social contract does or should work as the basis for state sovereignty. In this process, each contract is leant meaning by other contracts. Most significant for this study is the relationship between social and sexual contracts, but the employment contract also informs perceptions of *the Scene* due to its corporate aesthetic.

The social contract emerged in Europe during the seventeenth century. As a theory and a mythical object, the contract marks a break from monarchism in which social order is preordained and select people have a divine right to rule. Against monarchy, early contract theorists asserted inherent universal equality. To understand how "naturally free and equal" individuals would give up their autonomy and comply with the inequality of monarchical societies, contractarians theorised each "must, necessarily *agree* to be ruled" (Pateman 1988, 69 original emphasis). In Hobbes, legitimate agreement included that given under the threat of a sovereign's lethal power – the alternative to being ruled is death (Pateman 1988). The story of the social contract helped disrupt theologically justified monarchy and associated social inequality. It does this by theorising the legitimacy of consenting to submission in exchange for protection.

Subsequently, in narratives of eighteenth-century revolution, the social contract delivered people from the ingrained inequality of monarchy into political worlds of democracy (and ostensible equality). They were transformed from subjects to citizens. As citizens, individuals are imagined able to negotiate the terms of the social contract – to participate in decisions concerning the laws that they must obey, and which protect them. Through these stories, individuals are freed from obligatory social positions determined at birth (Naffine 1998, 196). And the social contract is established as "a means to secure and enhance individual freedom" (Pateman 1988, 102). Thus, while the social contract *explains* social inequality despite natural equality, it is also understood as a tool for *realising* equality.

Correspondingly, contracts are imagined to facilitate fair agreements between parties of unequal power. This is effective at the macro level with collective consent to a sovereign order (to be ruled), down to individualised negotiations over labour and remuneration (employment), and smaller still to relations between people in their private realms (marriage). In rape law, contracts are imagined in the most intimate of moments, so that best practice sex is conducted using informal contractual conversations. Contracts, from the broadest overarching societal to the most miniature of interpersonal agreements, simultaneously emerge from the assertion of universal equality while they also promise to create equality by mediating pre-existing power imbalances. The meaning of contracts more generally is shaped by social contract narratives.

In the context of rape law reform, reframing sex as ongoing contractual conversations was hoped to remove a burden from the complainant to prove their resistance to penetration (Powell et al. 2013, 462). The burden is theoretically relocated to the initiator/accused to evidence their "steps taken to find out whether the other person [was] consenting" (462). An initiator of sexual penetration is required to explicitly gain enthusiastic consent from the person they wish to penetrate and the penetratee is empowered to assert their desires on equal terms with the initiator. Contracts are imagined here to provide equality to possibly inequitable encounters.

While the social contract is deeply interwoven with ideas about equality, in this chapter I also examine autonomy and neutrality as liberal values associated with contract and consent. As part of the social contract landscape, they have also shaped contemporary rape law and, by extension, perceptions of sex. Equality, autonomy, and neutrality are signified in *the Scene*, enriching the contract romance plot with liberal feminist jurisprudence. As such, they make *the Scene* available to an optimistic, jurisprudential interpretation of sexual empowerment for a young, inexperienced woman.

Contractual Equality

An ostensibly transformed and newly empowered Ana is presented in a two-step reveal in the moments immediately prior to *the Scene* when the elevator doors open, and she removes her trench coat. The sequence echoes the much anticipated "after" moments in makeover reality programmes while also reprising a corresponding sequence within the film: the elevator ride directly preceding Ana's *first* meeting with Christian. The parallel between the two rides encourages consumers to note a contrast between the shy, frumpy, stumbling girl in floral shirt, floppy cardigan, heavy boots, and ponytail of the first, with the cool, poised woman in trench coat and chic hair of the second. Ana has metamorphosed into a *self-possessed* woman. Critical to this perception of transformation is the document file she holds. The object resonates with significance. This is what she is here to discuss; this is what contains the mystifying lists of sex acts and toys she has been shown reading with open-mouthed *naïveté* only a few scenes earlier. This object embodies the couple's negotiations over sex and romance at the heart of the film's narrative. The contract has become the tool through which Ana is able to name acts, toys, and conditions to which she is willing to "submit" while refusing others. The contract, in this scene, is presented as granting Ana the power to negotiate as an equal, her intimate relationship with the experienced and extraordinarily wealthy Christian.

The availability of the contract to be read as achieving equality is supported by *the Scene's* "corporate" aesthetic. This aesthetic is pre-empted by

Ana uttering "business meeting" as she and Christian enter the boardroom. The set is furnished with "executive" chairs around a "boardroom" table, filmed using neutrally angled wide shots that present a visual equivalence of power between them. The props include document files, luxury pens, and red tape. While the *mise-en-scène* bespeaks boardroom negotiations and employment contracts, Ana's costume presents her as professional, capable, and confident. Her dress mirrors Christian's suit as corporate attire – elegantly structured and tailored in suit fabric.

In this corporate context, the contract resembles an employment contract. Its structure and content seek to formalise the details of Ana's compliance with Christian's requirements. It lists the conditions to which Ana, as the consenting party, will be subject and the activities she will perform if she becomes a signatory. Employment contracts outline the duties prospective employees will perform, and their working conditions upon agreeing to a paid appointment. As employment contracts are understood to enable prospective employees to negotiate the terms of their employment, so Ana is shown agreeing to and refusing details within *the Scene's* contract. Then, like the promise of an executive bonus, Christian offers a "sweetener" in the form of weekly dates – morsels of the romance Ana desires – to make the proposed arrangement more favourable to her. While the dialogue presents Ana negotiating the conditions of a proposed relationship, *the Scene's* plot concludes with her walking away from an offer that she does not want. The contract empowers Ana to assert herself with an assurance she does not exercise anywhere else in the film in a fantasy echo of corporate employment negotiations. By invoking employment contracts, *the Scene* encourages us to read *its* contract as empowering for Ana.

Within social contract theory, employment contracts illustrate the capacity of contracts to facilitate negotiations between unequal parties. Inequality is assumed in a relationship between an employer, wealthy enough to pay for someone else's labour, and a person seeking a wage in exchange for their labour. Theoretically through their legal formality, employment contracts are a means for prospective employees to negotiate the work that they will perform, demand healthy and safe working environments and appropriate remuneration. They are supposed to protect employees from exploitation. Because of the distinctive power differential between employee and employer, the employment contract is "the exemplary contract" for theorising how agreements of mutual benefit and greater equality might be reached through formalised proposals and structures for recording consent or refusal (Pateman 1988, 97).

Despite the resemblance to an employment contract, *the Scene's* contract pertains to sex and sovereignty over Ana's life (eating, sleeping, drinking, working etc). However, such conflation of contract types exists across contract theory and popular understandings of what constitutes contracts generally. In this manner, the expectations and logic attached to employment contracts often transfer to assumptions about the social contract and marriage contracts, for example. Thus, when sex is reframed as contractual the navigation of intimacy can accumulate significances derived from the popular jurisprudence of employment contracts.

The most recent requirements in Victorian rape law – that an accused demonstrate they received enthusiastic consent before penetrating the complainant – consolidates a legal reframing of sex as contractual. Theoretically, the initiator of sex must be able to demonstrate they actively sought consent and that consent was given with enthusiasm (Powell et al. 2013). For penetration to *not* be rape, there needs to be a clear proposal to which the prospective penetratee may (withhold) consent. By extension and through the consent requirements of further sexual offences, sex is configured as an ongoing contractual conversation. Structurally unequal parties to sex are supported to negotiate sexual possibilities, including being able to refuse any or all proposed activities. Sex as contractual through rape law thus ideally protects the less powerful from coercion, exploitation, and violence. A trickle-down effect of contract and consent-based rape law reform has been an abundance of public education materials and school-based sexuality curricula emphasising consent (Burton et al. 2021; Beres 2020). Throughout these, it is understood that consent conversations enable the interests and concerns of less powerful parties to be heard and respected. Contracts here again promise to reduce inequality.

The contract in *Fifty Shades* enables Ana to assert herself despite her inexperience, youth, relative poverty, and lower social status in negotiating intimacy with a powerful man and even refusing him. Ultimately, she declines to sign the contract. She also refuses to have the sex Christian proposes. In this scene, Ana is Christian's equal. Her empowerment contrasts her disempowerment throughout the rest of the film. This is a rare instance in which Ana articulates consent or refusal, or when she refuses Christian without punishment or threat of punishment. Reading the contract as a positive tool that empowers Ana to assert herself as Christian's equal is supported by the inventory of liberal signifiers connoting stories of equality. The contract itself invokes liberal philosophical narratives in which contract and consent overcome inequality. These attach to the contract in *the Scene* and conspire with costuming, set design, and dialogue, allowing *the Scene* to be read through an optimistic liberal feminist lens.

Bodily Autonomy

Core to Ana's capacity to negotiate with Christian as his equal is autonomy. She is not seduced or coerced into signing the contract or having sex within *the Scene*. Further, she removes his hand from her body before the meeting even begins. Ana controls the contours of her body, demarcating its contact with other bodies. When she leaves the meeting, she has maintained those boundaries. In this moment she embodies the ideal subject of liberal legal philosophy as a "bounded individual entity that shields against 'unwanted intrusions'" (Urquiza-Haas 2017, 553). While the contract is represented as helping Ana maintain those boundaries, her characterisation in this scene as impenetrably autonomous is enhanced by her costume.

Contracts can be tools that enable individuals to police the boundaries of their bodies, making them autonomous legal subjects. The social contract facilitated "men [acquiring] mastery over their lives, over their bodies" following the dissolution of obligatory monarchical hierarchies (Naffine 1998, 203). Individuals are consequently configured as agents of their own destiny, able to negotiate and consent to the politico-legal order under which they live. Meanwhile, employees can ostensibly use contracts to set limitations on what they do with their bodies in exchange for a wage and demand protections to keep their bodies healthy and safe. The capacity to decide what our bodies experience and do is valued by liberal philosophy and contracts are critical tools for achieving and protecting such autonomy.

Correspondingly, when consent became the transformative kernel distinguishing legitimate penetrative sex from a criminal act, rape became an offence against individual autonomy. Cowan (2007, 92) explains that "rape is defined in terms of a violation of sexual autonomy and choice, that is the lack of consent." The harm of rape is the breaching of an individual's right to govern themselves and a defilement of their bodily integrity. Because "consent" represents free and voluntary agreement within a democracy, consent epitomises "the activities of an autonomous (legal) subject" (Hunter and Cowan 2007, 1). The fundamental status of consent in sexual offence law presumes a state of autonomy borne by all parties in a sexual encounter. At the same time, the legal requirement of consent makes legitimate sex contractual. The liberal subject is thus supported to self-govern, and to make rational, independent decisions about the sexual penetration of their body by contract and consent.

Congruent with contracts' association with autonomy, the highly developed "hard bodies" of bodybuilder heroes in 1980s action cinema epitomised and celebrated the impenetrable autonomous ideal of liberalism (Jeffords 1994). The contemporaneous political climate included perceived communist threats against US freedoms escalated injection-drug use, and panic concerning the emergence of a disease associated with penetrative (anal) sex, drug use, and blood transfusion. In this context, Silvester Stallone and Arnold Schwarzenegger became two of the most iconic actors in some of the most successful Hollywood films. The two competed publicly over their musculature and the prowess of their characters (Pearson 2017). While their characters performed the political ideals of "strength, labour, determination, loyalty and courage" – in line with the then right-wing President Reagan – the hardened outer shell of their extreme musculature exemplified the impenetrability of liberal autonomy (Jeffords 1994, 67). Presented as impervious to the temptation of injection drugs, "disease, fatigue or ageing," these characters were depicted as simultaneously embodying and defending liberal values (67). Concurrently, they manifest a "certain notion of individualism in which the individual . . . owns the narrative and therefore the sequence that it articulates" (67). These characters drove the narratives of their films through the exercise of their autonomy, and their capacity to govern themselves and make agentic decisions that directly contributed to the success of their endeavours in protecting their nation and liberal freedoms. Most significantly for Jeffords (1994), impenetrable autonomous individuality was manifest in the *hardness* of the actor/characters' bodies.

Contrastingly, throughout most of *Fifty Shades*, Ana's clothes are generally soft, displaying cleavage, and revealing legs. She wears florals, loose cardigans, scarves, and escaping wisps of hair. Compared with the hard bodies of Stallone and Schwarzenegger, this is a "soft" feminine body. Politically, it is like the left-leaning "leaky bodies" with their "liberal tears" that hard-right US liberals find so repugnant (Duncan 2017, 517).

However, in *the Scene* Ana's sheath dress presents a smooth surface that skates over the contours of her body (suggestive but not revealing). Consistent with Jefford's (1994) "hard bodies," Ana's dress imbues her character with political significance. "Sheath" refers to a protective coating that envelopes something. It is another name for condoms – the prophylactics that protect vaginas and anuses from sperm and sexually transmitted diseases during penetration. Correspondingly, while Ana's softly costumed body capitulates and is penetrated by Christian's desires, Ana's sheathed body has a harder boundary resistant to such penetration. Ana's impenetrably sheathed body, like Jefford's "hard bodies," is granted autonomy and exercises agency. Although she is otherwise a relatively passive narrative subject and the object of Christian's pursuit, in *the Scene* Ana leads the narrative: she takes control by verbally extending Christian's sexual fantasy and then declines it. She refuses to allow him to rewrite her non-consent when he reads desire on the surfaces of her body. She exerts ultimate control by finishing the meeting and exiting. Her sleek appearance bespeaks an impenetrability that aligns with her resistance to penetration: not signing the contract and not "being fucked" on the table.

Sound contributes to Ana's perceived autonomy. Throughout *the Scene* playful violins and xylophone mix with more serious and tense strings. These diminish to give dominance to the sound of stilettos hitting hard floor denoting Ana's exit. Stilettos are semiotically paradoxical because of the difficulty they present to walking whilst simultaneously symbolising feminine sexual power. Primarily, they are conventionally sexy. The crisp clarity of their soundscape in this fleeting moment emphatically invokes the fantastical power associated with an ostensibly sexually available woman who says no to sex. Ana's autonomy is endorsed through the bodily pleasure of consumers hearing her exit. This pleasure is associated with the contract as a tool to establish boundaries within a heterosexual relationship.

Gender Neutrality

The last liberal feminist value I trace in *the Scene* is neutrality. Often represented by Lady Justice's blindfold, law's "blindness" to difference promises fairness through impartiality. Gender neutralisation in law has significantly altered employment, family, and sexual offence law, reducing the singularised control wielded by husbands and fathers (patriarchs) within families, contributing towards de-gendering parental roles, granting women greater property rights and broadening women's employment opportunities (Saguy et al. 2020). Rape law has been a particular site of gender-neutralising reform. In *the Scene*, while the contract implements gender-neutral language, the *mise-en-scène* and costuming textures the corporate aesthetic with "neutral" significance.

Contract theory relies on the concept of neutrality, which presumes that by removing or obscuring markers of difference, associated power differentials might be reduced or eliminated. In overtly gendered fields of law, this is more obvious. For example, in some jurisdictions gendered terms like "mother" and "wife" have been removed from family law and replaced with seemingly neutral terms "parent" and "spouse" (Boshoff 2007, 42). In this manner, Boshoff (42) observes, that the concept of "woman" "seems to be successfully freed from the liberal notion of sexualised dualism." Legal expectations are no longer tied to gender, thus better-enabling flexibility within the roles people perform within families.

Rape law has been an important focus of gender neutralisation due to its history as a specifically gendered crime. While a range of offences from antiquity concerned men "lying with" or "ravishing" virginal women, in eighteenth-century England, rape was defined as "carnal knowledge of a woman forcibly and against her will" (Blackstone 1826, 238). Currently in the United Kingdom, rape requires that the penetration involve "his penis" (*Sexual Offences Act 2003*). However, anuses and mouths now join vaginas as sites of potentially unlawful penetration. Within two years of the reform, the first case involving a male complainant reached court (Javaid 2018). Meanwhile, Victoria has expanded the category of penetrating articles to include other body parts and inanimate objects (*Crimes (Sexual Offences) Act* 1991). By breaking from the model of rape as an offence perpetrated by a man with a penis against a woman with a vagina, Victorian legislation no longer requires survivors and perpetrators conform to gender binaries. Women can be perpetrators and men survivors. But also, recognition of trans* and non-binary people as victims/survivors or perpetrators of rape is now possible. A considerable amount of sexual violence against LGBTQ* people has been obscured in part because of the history of rape as a gendered crime (Patterson 2016; Ison 2020). As rape has transformed into a crime about autonomy, so its gender neutralisation has made it relevant beyond the heteronormative.

On one level, by making rape gender-neutral, women can be recognised as wielding not simply the physical capacity, cultural capital, or socio-economic authority to overpower or coercively force another person to penetrate them against their will (Naffine 1994, 24). At a deeper level, gender neutrality potentially expands women's role beyond the recipient of sexual invitations and allows us to better imagine women as initiators of sex. Part of the heteronormativity limiting traditional rape law is the configuration of men as agents (active legal subjects) who *do* penetrative sex *to* women. Meanwhile, women are configured as recipients who might say yes or no, or passively oblige. Women's status in pre-reform rape law corresponds with women's marital status prior to the late nineteenth century. Married women lost their ability to own property, including control of their bodies as property, and could not be recognised by law except as part of their husband's household (Naffine 1994). Through gender-neutralisation women can be imagined as owners of property (including their own bodies), initiators of sex, agents acting on their own desires – sometimes causing harm to others. Liberalism's gender neutrality provides the possibility for imagining women as legal subjects equivalent to men.

The gender neutrality of *the Scene's* contract contributes to Ana's empowerment to act as an agent of her own desires. The neutrality is presented in a shot establishing the document as a contract. Capitalised lettering asserts the contracting parties: "the DOMINANT" and "the SUBMISSIVE." Instead of gender-indicative names, or gendered titles (husband and wife), the contractors become abstracted roles. As such, the contract reiterates the gender neutrality of reformed rape law and in this manner works with the potentially universally applicable "sexually neuter category of the 'individual'" (Pateman 1988, 72). Using this tool – through which Ana's condition as "feminine" and as the object of Christian's gaze and desire, is reduced – Ana can exercise her agency, police the boundaries of her body as an autonomous legal subject and refuse both sex and contract.

The neutralising effect of the contract's language is echoed in *the Scene's mise-en-scène* and Ana's costuming. I will return to the architectural semiotics of neutrality in the next chapter. However, it is important to note the absence of decoration in the room, the lack of carpet, art, or ornamental detail in the furnishing. Such absence is meaningful in legal architecture and is used to signify and promote neutrality as the absence of representations of difference (Henderson and Duncanson 2019; Duncanson and Henderson 2022). It is assumed that this will provide greater equality to legal process. The same significance is encouraged in *the Scene* by the use of "neutral" wide shots in which Ana and Christian are presented level, at opposite ends of a long table.

Meanwhile, Ana's dress as "corporate attire" – tailored in suiting fabric – is a feminised version of the male business suit. As the material skims Ana's frame, sheathing her soft curves with a firm outer shell, it resembles the "easy-fitting sheath" of the male suit, hiding "the body's whole surface quite thoroughly" with a solid block of colour (Hollander 2016, 83). Hollander (83) contrasts mid-1990s suits with a contextual fashion era of "trained muscles and near nudity." Similarly, Ana's dress contrasts the extensive nudity, soft blouses, and revealing décolletages of the surrounding film, rendering the sheath dress more masculine and corporate. Such juxtaposition supports suits' "reputation of being inexpressive" (83). Goodall (2013 *emphasis added*) contends that suits "*standardise the personal silhouette*, creating smooth, subdued outlines." In this vein of inexpressive, standardisation of bodies, suits are often perceived as *uniform* (Hollander 2016). Suits appear to bear a neutrality as a uniform that makes everyone the same. In the context of childhood education, it is argued that bullying is circumvented because "uniforms are social and economic equalizers, which reduce opportunities for children to criticize others on . . . appearance" (Hassan 2014). School uniforms were introduced to English schools to camouflage class differences and equalise perceived social differences (Craik 2005, 230). Discernible in this reasoning are the assumptions that a universal design will render homogeneity across differentiation and that equality issues from the suppression of visual signifiers of diversity. As suit-like corporate attire, Ana's dress signifies neutrality.

By reducing the feminine (smoothing over curves, covering legs, minimising decolletage) and increasing the masculine (tailoring, fabric, coverage) the dress provides a neutrality that grants Ana access to agentic legal subjecthood. The wardrobing of leading female politicians in the West, from Margaret Thatcher to Angela Merkel, evidences the use of suits as gender-neutralising uniforms (Goodall 2013). Julia Gillard, Australia's first woman Prime Minister, described her suits as "a uniform" (Freedman 2010). She explains that her central wardrobe goal was to redirect attention from her clothes and her femaleness to matters of state (Hadfield 2013). Meanwhile, Hillary Clinton explained her US presidential campaign *pantsuit* as a "visual cue" of sameness with male politicians (Clinton 2017, 88). *Vogue* explains that women's pantsuits are "intentionally unfeminine" and do not "engage with sexuality" (Satenstein 2016). Suits ostensibly downplay gender differences. Following this theory, suits render women visually equivalent to men as potentially consummate politico-legal subjects: democratic heads of state. In the second feminist reading of *the Scene*, I investigate the way womanliness can be read as exaggerated, abject, and queer in its resistance to containment by the suit silhouette. However, women's corporate attire significantly marks the entrance of women into the public spheres of business, law, and politics in its resemblance to the male suit "uniform" (Hollander 2016). Corporate attire thus signifies the capacity of a woman to function as a legal subject who can self-govern as well as potentially govern others. In this way, Ana's sheath dress connotes the "sexless representative" promised by contract theory (Pateman 1988, 74). As an echo of the suit, the dress empowers Ana as an agentic legal subject through the neutralisation of her gender.

Ana's empowered agentic subjecthood plays out through her collaboration with Christian's sexual fantasy. Although she doesn't initiate it, she extends the fantasy both by building onto its sensuality – pressing her palm into the tabletop while asking if he will do it "right here?" Within the context of the corporate *mise-en-scène* and the couple's respective "suits," Ana touching the table is available to be read as an exercise of the agency granted by the contract's gender neutrality. This is a feminist legal argument that contracts can empower women to better negotiate heterosexual intimacy.

Empowered by Contract and Consent

Ana's refusal to sign and to have sex within *the Scene* evidences the power of contracts to facilitate greater equality and autonomy for women as a marginalised group. In contrast to her previous capitulation (rather than active consent) to Christian's initiations throughout the rest of the film, Ana's capacity to say "no" is demonstrated explicitly in the context of a contract. The coincidence of Ana's refusal with a contract makes cinematic jurisprudence easier to see. In this chapter, I have demonstrated the way that the liberal values of equality, autonomy, and gender neutrality, are signified by the *mise-en-scène*, costuming, narrative, and dialogue. These values support an optimistic liberal feminist legal argument that contracts and consent can empower women to navigate heterosexual intimacy.

Law is present within this brief scene. Its presence is not neutral but shaped by ideas about what law is and how it works. Specific cultural values are made available through *the Scene*, guiding consumers to understand law in particular ways. I suggest that one dominant reading offered is optimistic, liberal, and feminist – hopeful that through gender neutrality contracts and consent can grant women access to equality and autonomy with which they may achieve agentic legal subjecthood, enabling them to police the boundaries of their bodies while enjoying interesting sex.

A feminist liberal legal interpretation is endorsed by a *frisson* offered within *the Scene*. In my *Third Reading: Legal Sensations* I demonstrate how sound and arousal reach out to consumers of this cinematic moment, inviting them to lose themselves to sensation. Liberal feminist values texture those sensations, providing them with legal significance. While the naming of sex acts and toys might be thrilling, tight shots of parted lips and pencil nibbling – backed by building musical tension – foster arousal, which is then abruptly (triumphantly) frustrated by Ana's exit. The dress contributes to the sense of victory in its sexy reference to powerful women Elegant and alluring in its body-skimming sheath, Ana's dress animates liberal values with its demurely tantalising suggestion of the figure within. Ana's feminist liberal legal empowerment is *felt* in the thrill of delayed sexual gratification.

But first I want to demonstrate that there is more than one theory of law available in *the Scene*. By demonstrating that *the Scene* can also be read through a pessimistic poststructural feminist legal analysis, I am building evidence that consumers are grappling with different possible interpretations of law while watching film.

Bibliography

Beres, Melanie. (2020). Perspectives of Rape-Prevention Educators on the Role of Consent in Sexual Violence Prevention. *Sex Education*, 20(2), pp. 227–238.

Blackstone, William. (1826). *Commentaries on the Laws of England, Volume* 2. William Walker.

Boshoff, Anél. (2007). Woman as the Subject of (Family) Law. In Hunter, Rosemary, and Cowan, Sharon (Eds). *Choice and Consent: Feminist Engagements with Law and Subjectivity.* (pp. 41–57). Routledge-Cavendish.

Burton, Olivia, Rawstorne, Patrick, Watchirs-Smith, Lucy, Nathan, Sally, and Carter, Allison. (2021). Teaching Sexual Consent to Young People in Education Settings: A Narrative Systematic Review. *Sex Education*, 23(1), pp. 18–34.

Clinton, Hilary. (2017). *What Happened.* Simon and Schuster.

Cott, Nancy. (2002). *Public Vows: A History of Marriage and the Nation.* Harvard University Press.

Cowan, Sharon. (2007). Choosing Freely: Theoretically Reframing the Concept of Consent. In Hunter, Rosemary, and Cowan, Sharon (Eds). *Choice and Consent: Feminist Engagements with Law and Subjectivity* (pp. 91–105). Routledge-Cavendish.

Craik, Jennifer. (2005). *Exposed: From Conformity to Transgression: Dress, Body, Culture.* Berg Publishers.

Crimes (Sexual Offences) Act 1991 Victoria.

Douglas, Heather. (2008). Stories of Mistaken Consent: Still in the Shadow of *Morgan*. In Hunter, Rosemary, and Cowan, Sharon (Eds). *Choice and Consent: Feminist Engagements with Law and Subjectivity* (pp. 109–124). Routledge-Cavendish.

Duncan, Pansy. (2017). "I Drink Liberal Tears": Genre Desire and the Leaky Liberal Body. *Feminist Media Studies*, 17(3), pp. 516–520.

Duncanson, Kirsty, and Henderson, Emma. (2022). Interpellation by Design: Could Court Buildings Influence Jury Decision Making. In Duncanson, Kirsty, and Henderson, Emma (Eds). *Court Architecture, Design and Social Justice* (pp. 107–139). Routledge.

Freedman, Mia. (August 2, 2010). Critiquing Julia's Clothes is Wearing Thin. *Sydney Morning Herald.* www.smh.com.au/politics/federal/critiquing-julias-clothes-is-wearing-thin-20100802-111pf.html

Goodall, Jane. (April 26, 2013). Dressing the Part: Women, Power, Fashion and that Bloody Jacket. *The Conversation.* https://theconversation.com/dressing-the-part-women-power-fashion-and-that-bloody-jacket-13659

Hadfield, Shelley. (April 17, 2013). Julia Gillard Laughs off the Continuing Attention to Her Wardrobe. *news.com.au.* www.news.com.au/national/julia-gillard-laughs-off-the-continuing-attention-to-her-wardrobe/news-story/761567f0e4fb496f967f3116ba12f7d2

Hassan, Farzana. (September 18, 2014). School Uniforms will Help Stop Bullying. *Toronto Sun*. https://torontosun.com/2014/09/18/school-uniforms-will-help-stop-bullying
Henderson, Emma, and Kirsty Duncanson. (2019). Design and Ideology – Innovation in the Magistrates' Court. *Griffith Law Review*, 27(2), pp. 207–232.
Hollander, Anne. (2016). *Sex and Suits: The Evolution of Modern Dress*. Bloomsbury.
Hunter, Rosemary, and Cowan, Sharon. (2007). *Choice and Consent: Feminist Engagements with Law and Subjectivity*. Routledge-Cavendish.
Ison, Jess. (2020). "It's Not Just Men and Women": LGBTQIA People and #MeToo'. In Loney-Howes, Rachel, and Fileborn, Bianca (Eds). *#MeToo and the Politics of Social Change* (pp. 151–167). Palgrave MacMillan.
Javaid, Aliraza. (2018). *Male Rape, Masculinities and Sexualities: Understanding, Policing and Overcoming Male Sexual Victimisation*. Palgrave Macmillan.
Jeffords, Susan. (1994). *Hard Bodies: Hollywood Masculinity in the Reagan Era*. Rutgers University Press.
Munro, Vanessa. (2008). Constructing Consent: Legislating Freedom and Legitimating Constraint in the Expression of Sexual Autonomy. *Akron Law Review*, 41, pp. 923–956.
Naffine, Ngaire. (1994). Possession: Erotic Law and the Law of Rape. *Modern Law Review*, 57, pp. 10–37.
Naffine, Ngaire. (1998). The Legal Structure of Self-Ownership: Or the Self-Possessed Man and the Woman Possessed. *Journal of Law and Society*, 25(2), pp. 193–212.
Pateman, Carol. (1988). *The Sexual Contract*. Polity Press.
Patterson, Jennifer. (2016). *Queering Sexual Violence: Radical Voices from within the Anti-Violence Movement*. Riverdale Avenue Books.
Pearson, Ben. (2017). Arnold Schwarzenegger Confirmed One of Hollywood's All-Time Great Troll Moves in a Fantastic Q&A. *Slashfilm.com*. www.slashfilm.com/553774/arnold-schwarzenegger-beyond-fest/
Powell, Anastasia, Henry, Nicola, Henderson, Emma, and Flynn, Asher. (2013). The Meanings of "Sex" and "Consent": History, Discourse and Impact of Rape Law Reform in Victoria (Australia). *Griffith Law Review*, 22(2), pp. 456–480.
Saguy, Abigail C., Williams, Juliet A., and Rees, Mallory. (2020). Reassessing Gender Neutrality. *Law and Society Review*, 54(3), pp. 743–743.
Satenstein, Liana. (November, 2016). Wearing the Pantsuit: One Vogue.com Writer Goes Looking for the Hillary Clinton Effect. *Vogue*. www.vogue.com/article/pantsuit-hillary-clinton-effect
Sexual Offences Act 2003 *(c. 42)* UK.
Taylor-Johnson, Samantha (Director). (2015). *Fifty Shades of Grey* [Film] Focus Features, Michael De Luca Productions, Trigger Street Productions, Universal Pictures.
Urquiza-Haas, Nayeli. (2017). The Semiotic Fractures of Vulnerable Bodies: Resistance to the Gendering of Legal Subjects. *International Journal for the Semiotics of Law*, 30, pp. 543–562.

Second Reading

The Discomforts of Subordination

Even as the gender neutrality and empowerment of women's entry into the public sphere can be affectively registered through the allure of Ana's dress, that allure also signifies the impossibility of full female agency within liberalism offered by contracts and consent. Much of the dress' charm is reliant on the misalignment of the female body with liberal ideals: a significant part of what makes it sexy is its feminisation of the masculine suit. By the dress cinching at the waist, accommodating Ana's curves, the non-compliance of her body with the suit-silhouette is emphasised. This dissonance creates a bodily delight. As such, the dress echoes an excitement in *the Scene* from *Fifty Shades of Grey* (Taylor-Johnson 2015) derived from Ana momentarily exerting agency, refusing both sex and contract. It is thrilling because it *briefly* reverses the order of things. However, the tantalisingly fleeting quality of her agency potentially entrenches her subordination. This is a second interpretation of *the Scene:* a pessimistic poststructuralist feminist legal critique, reading paradoxical subjugation within the promises enjoyed by my first, optimistic *liberal* feminist analysis.

A central purpose of this chapter is to demonstrate that more than one legal theory is available in *the Scene*. Poststructuralism interrogates and disrupts liberal philosophy. As such, poststructural and liberal feminisms are ostensible adversaries. I emphasise this with my opposing optimistic and pessimistic readings. Rather than trumping one reading with a truer insight, I insist that a single feminist can engage with both readings simultaneously. I am proof of this. By establishing a counter reading, I present evidence that consumers evaluate multiple available legal arguments as they watch. Consuming cinema involves experimenting with different possible ways of understanding law or performing legal theory. In my third reading of *the Scene*, I build on these ideas to demonstrate that theorising law at the cinema involves consumer-bodies.

This chapter begins with a curated explanation of poststructuralist feminist jurisprudence. Poststructuralist feminists have argued that contract and consent are false promises of liberal legalism, particularly in the context of rape law, which further entrench inequality and prevent survivors from realising justice. The analysis of this chapter identifies a series of paradoxes within

DOI: 10.4324/9780429330414-7

the liberal values of gender neutrality, autonomy, and equality celebrated in my first reading. Ultimately this interpretation finds contract and consent in *the Scene* relies on a residual history of strongly gendered liberal jurisprudence which continues to marginalise women as a category of legal person and undermines the potential empowerment it offers.

Feminist Poststructuralist Legal Critique and Rape Law

To establish a working definition of poststructuralist feminism some basic knowledge of structuralism is useful. Structuralist analysis exposes "deep structures" shaping and supporting communication, knowledge and social relationships in the human world (Scales 2009, 395). These are patterns, categorisations, and rules that appear to persist across cultures and time. My semiotic cinematic analysis relies on Saussure's structuralist linguistics which uncovered a hidden system undergirding language. Adapting Saussurean linguistics for social science, Levis-Strauss identified persistent patterns within myths and rituals and human behaviour across multiple cultures, revealing shared symbolic structures. He produced profound insights into human community and established influential methods for analysing culture (Kurzweil 2017, 1). Based on his discovery of similarities across cultures, he made significant generalisations about culture he believed held true over time.

Although for many, structuralism uncovers universal and essential human patterns, for others, it reveals that phenomena we experience as unquestionably logical or natural are culturally created. In the example of Saussure's linguistics, he revealed a distinction between language as an abstract system of representation and an external reality. The relationship between words and reality was denaturalised. Language came to be seen as a cultural construction *representing* reality. This is fundamental to poststructuralist thought.

Poststructuralism builds on, while also departing from, structuralism. While it too investigates deep structures, poststructuralism goes further, revelling in discrepancies, inconsistencies, and paradoxes within and between structures. Suspicious of truth claims and generalisations, poststructuralists treat discrepancies as evidence that deep structures are not universal and alternative knowledges and ways of knowing are possible. Thus, in the linguistically denaturalised relationship between words and things, no external reality or truth is unveiled because there is no escape from representation. Instead, discrepancies and paradoxes reveal how structures are "linguistically, culturally and psychologically 'constructed'" (Scales 2009, 404).

While language and "the underlying structures of language" are particular preoccupations for poststructuralism, so too is knowledge generated through liberal philosophy and enlightenment methods (Papadelos 2010, 37). As an embodiment of deep structures, powerfully dependent on language, and woven through with liberal philosophy, law is a rich site of poststructuralist critique.

Law relies on, creates, recreates, and applies categories: setting boundaries, establishing distinctions, instituting and policing rules and formulas for discovering truth. Poststructuralism has demonstrated "the importance of language in framing legal institutions, legal categories, and definitions" of gender, sex and sexuality, race, class, and ableness, for example (Stacey 1996, 116). Liberalism is at work throughout this system, enhancing category dependence with presumptions of universality and equality, insisting on reason, objectivity, and neutrality. A significant purpose of law is to establish singular *truths* from disputed events, acts, subjecthood, and relationships. In its adherence to established methods for discovering binary truth/untruth (guilty/not guilty), law parallels enlightenment scientific knowledge production (Smart 1990). Meanwhile, poststructuralism reveals the lack of objectivity in law's methods, exposing the preferred interests of law that masquerade as "disinterested neutrality" (Stacey 1996, 121). Although structuralists demonstrate the gap between law's structures and the reality of the world beyond, in poststructuralism there is "nothing beyond the world of human discourse to stand on when participating in social life, including participation in law and philosophy" (Scales 2009, 405). Law is one of the mechanisms mediating how we perceive reality. Textured by liberalism, law embodies the "deep structures" poststructuralism critiques.

Feminists have contributed significantly to poststructuralism by mapping and interrogating gendered power working throughout the deep structures. The previous chapter, *Reader Agency*, surveyed poststructuralist feminist cultural scholarship revealing the maligning of women's fiction, infantilisation of its consumers, and suppression of women's agency. While exposing the ways women's voices are buried by patriarchal discourses, poststructuralist feminists also "seek a voice for 'Woman' which can be heard . . . beyond male representations of desire" (Stacey 1996, 121). For example, in Kristeva's (1984, 2000) work, while masculine discourses dominate, feminine experiences exceed, cannot be contained, and are expressed in ways that defy patriarchal structures. Feminist poststructuralism critiques dominant discourses and language for patterns of exclusion, practices of domination, discrepancies, and paradoxes, while also drawing out, celebrating, and exploring those discourses that subvert, resist, and express alternative knowledges and experiences.

A persistent endeavour of poststructuralist feminist legal theorists involves interrogating falling conviction rates for rape despite liberal feminist law reform. For example, Smart (1990) demonstrates the "scientific" method law implements to test evidence at trial and establish a singular "true" finding. Due to its gendered structure, the method silences complainants' voices and "proves" each complaint "false." Young (1998) deconstructs the linguistic formulation of cross-examination, revealing the manipulation of complainant testimony to imply consent. I have interrogated passive voice and agentic syntax mitigating men's responsibility for sexual and fatal violence in legal judgment (Duncanson 2014). Naffine (1998) shows how the gendered violence of liberal philosophy is woven into rape law, particularly expectations of embodied subjecthood and the ability to be recognised or heard by law to refuse consent. Meanwhile, Cowan (2007), Munro (2008) and Du Toit (2007, 2009) have demonstrated the gendered signification of "consent" and the implications for rape complainants. For each feminist, the deep structures of law, its linguistic practices, and incorporation of liberal philosophy are critiqued. Repeatedly, consent and the contractual quality of contemporary rape law are revealed as obstacles rather than empowering tools for women navigating heterosexual intimacy.

Poststructuralist feminist legal critique unveils paradoxes at the heart of neutrality and autonomy – values core to consent and contract. Both rely on an ideal model of subjecthood which aligns with privileged masculinities. Thus, a poststructuralist feminist legal interpretation of *the Scene* reads in its signifiers of neutrality, autonomy, and equality persistent evidence of gendered subordination and violence, silencing experiences of sexual violence and obstructing women's agency. Ultimately, this second reading argues that Ana's non-consent in *the Scene* functions perversely to render Ana responsible for the violence to which she is subject throughout the rest of the film. I begin by looking at the way in which neutrality functions in *the Scene* to paradoxically accentuate Ana's divergence from the liberal legal ideal of subjecthood and thereby hinders her access to contract and consent.

Paradoxical Neutrality

A paradox lies at the heart of neutrality. Rather than establishing equality by reducing markers of difference, neutrality provides a set of culturally specific criteria which few bodies meet. Despite hopes that de-gendering language and mandating uniforms increase equivalence, a hidden template persists and those who do not align are marginalised. Simultaneously, insistence on neutrality obscures the structural design of exclusion and situates responsibility with the bodies that do not conform. Counter to the earlier liberal feminist interpretation, *the Scene's* key signifiers of neutrality – the contract, dress, and *mise-en-scène* – are read in this chapter as undermining Ana's capacity to negotiate heterosexual intimacy.

Overcoming inequality by reducing markers of difference is characteristic of liberal law reform (Stacey 1996). Removing gendered words is thought to "unproblematically" open the hitherto masculine subjectivity of law "to also include the female" (Boshoff 2007). In contemporary social contract theory, where parties to the contract were once "sexually differentiated," there is now an "apparently universal, sexually neuter category of the 'individual'" (Pateman 1988, 72). The neutrality of contracts more generally promises to mitigate power differentials between parties. Meanwhile, the removal of gendered language in rape law has technically granted greater access to justice for survivors beyond its previously explicitly gendered definitions. Gender neutrality appears to have rendered legal subjecthood universal.

The neutering of legal language is referenced by *the Scene's* capitalised titling of the parties to its contract. Instead of gender-indicative names, the contractors become abstract roles: "the DOMINANT" and "the SUBMISSIVE." The contracted power dynamic appears disconnected from systemic subordination, manifesting instead as mutually agreed-upon functions. Ana's dress also signifies neutrality. Women's corporate attire echoes masculine business suits by replicating form, coverage and fabric. Suits ostensibly neutralise the impact of difference by hiding bodies within a uniform silhouette (Goodall 2013). Concurrently, *the Scene's* unadorned walls and absence of clutter make the *mise-en-scène* ostensibly unencumbered by cultural value. The uniformity of corporate design in architecture, interior design, and costuming promises to reduce subjective variance in the public realm and enhance equality through neutrality (Crawford 2009; Duncanson and Henderson 2022).

However, on closer (poststructuralist) inspection, each example invokes an ideal to which bodies must conform to gain subjecthood. Accordingly, *the Scene's* blank walls echo modernist architecture, the philosophy of which associates ornamentation with "the feminine" as "masquerade" and "artifice" (Crawford 2009, 20). Blank walls are aesthetically meaningful and "orderliness" holds cultural value (Duncanson and Henderson 2022). Concurrently, the homogeneity of suits accentuates physical variance rather than disguising it. Hollander (2016) demonstrates this in the contrast between suits and ballgowns in impressionist art: while women are rendered a blur of ruffles and colour, men's faces stand out, individualised against their otherwise identical suits. Varied decorative costume pulls the eye to colour and texture, deemphasising the idiosyncrasies of each person while uniforms provide a consistent foundation against which difference is made visible.

Bodily signifiers of "womanhood" are regularly accentuated by suits' inflexible inverted-triangle (masculine) silhouette. The divergence discernible in a woman wearing a suit creates dissonance: a tension generated through conflict between the costume's structure and the body within. Emphasised are ways in which the bodily form "woman" does not "fit." This is sexualised by pencil skirts clinging to curvaceous thighs and bottoms; shirts, jackets, and waistcoats bursting at busts; sexy décolletages dramatizing breasts and diaphanous blouses and pussy-bows as exaggerated feminine embellishments. More androgynous suiting might better replicate the masculine silhouette, yet sexed *affect* is not necessarily neutralised nor is the body within straightforwardly empowered. Disjuncture remains. Since at least *Deuteronomy* 2:55, laws have prohibited people designated female from wearing men's garments. Such law sentenced Joan of Arc's death in 1431 because she refused to "stop dressing as a man" (Feinberg 2006, 212–214). In Renaissance England, women "dressed as men" were "corrected" as "sexual transgressors" with whipping, pillorying, and imprisonment (Saccardi 2018, 65). From 1848 to the mid-twentieth century, most US states criminalised gender non-conforming dressing (Stryker 2008; Sears 2015). Throughout Western history, cross-gendered dressing has troubled law. Meantime, women's corporate fashion regularly accentuates rather than minimises bodily signifiers used to distinguish the gender binary.

Suit "fit" is commonly conflated with "fitting" subjecthood. This is exemplified by democratic discourses concerning women's participation (Goodall 2013). Even as Hilary Clinton declared the important equivalence signified by her pantsuit between herself and male opponents during her presidential campaign, she noted it also signalled her difference from them (Clinton 2017). Pantsuits mark Clinton's anatomical divergence from the traditional male form of the United States presidency. Further, her body became "central to how her opponents viewed her" (Clemente 2016). Explicit references to her thighs and breasts emblazoned Republican campaign badges. Whereas the wardrobes of male politicians rarely attract comment, Clinton's pantsuits received attention in political and "apolitical" commentary alike (Freedman 2010). Columns in *The Conversation* (Clemente 2016) and *Wired* (Pandell 2016) focused on her clothes while *Vogue* struggled with her pantsuits as a social phenomenon that empowered women but "lacked femininity" in a column that ultimately provided tips for making pantsuits sexy (Satenstein 2016). The pantsuit became emblematic of Clinton's campaign as an embodiment of "woman" in the public realm. It evidenced her nonalignment with the idealised embodiment of liberal subjecthood.

Correspondingly in Australia, public feminist intellectual Germaine Greer advised Prime Minister Gillard, on national television, against her suit uniform because of her "big arse" (*The Sydney Morning Herald* 2012). Greer instructed Gillard to "get over it" and accept the suits "don't fit" (Goodall 2013). Compellingly, the problem identified by Greer is a significantly sexualised body part which is *too much* (too big) for the "universal" silhouette. Rather than being neutralised by the suit uniform, Gillard's sexed difference cannot be contained by it. Her body won't fit the liberal model of subjecthood. Like the suit, neutrality's promise of equality through reduced signifiers of difference has a fundamental shape which numerous bodies do not "fit." Accordingly, access to legal subjecthood is constrained.

Correspondingly, gender-neutralising law reform appears superficial because it misses deep structural configurations of sex and subjecthood. Hence, replacing "mother" and "wife" with gender-neutral terms "parent" and "partner" in family law has not altered the "fundamental structure of the legal subject" (Boshoff 2007, 53). The required attributes remain masculine, and law continues to privilege cis-gendered male (ex)partners and parents at the cost of others. Gender-neutralised law "does not fit our political, legal, emotional or intuitive experiences" (Boshoff 2007, 53). The ideal attributes of subjecthood do not extend to accommodate many women's (and Others') experiences of family.

Similarly, despite the hope offered by rape law reform to improve recognition of sexual violence, rape convictions dropped across the common law world throughout the early twenty-first century (Larcombe 2011). Broadening legal categories of *who* can penetrate *whom* without consent has not fully enabled law to recognise women's agency nor understand when women say no. Neither has gender-neutralisation overcome broader inequalities (economic, political, representational . . .) that render women (and many others) vulnerable to sexual violence. For poststructuralist feminists, gender neutrality does not penetrate deeply enough to realise better outcomes for survivors of sexual violence. The inability of law to recognise when women contract or refuse consent persists because women's bodies do not "fit" the criteria of neutered legal subjecthood.

Meanwhile, insistence on neutrality obscures the specificity of liberal legal subjecthood and obfuscates structural impediments to equality. The gender-neutral paradigm persistently ignores struggles unique to specific groups of persons who do not conform (Ammaturo 2018). The distinct textures of sexual violence experienced along gendered lines are obscured. Power dynamics rendering some groups more vulnerable to violence disappear, while structural impediments to accessing legal remedies (such as historically manifest criminalisation of divergent gender and sexual expression) are hidden. Although gender neutrality offers the theoretical possibility of prosecuting harms perpetrated against cis-men, non-binary, and trans* people as well as cis-women, the same universal framework of subjecthood is required of each complainant. Thus, although the category of "rape victim" is formally expanded, the structural requirements for victims/survivors continue inhibiting access to justice for those who don't "fit."

Poststructuralist feminists have argued that women's bodies do not "fit" subjecthood because liberal theory relies on the subjugation of women – particularly through the philosophical configuration of women as sexual objects (Naffine 1994, 1998; Du Toit 2007, 2009). Pateman (1988, 90) names a "sexual contract" through which social contract theorists exclude women "from participation in the original contract." Early philosophers, such as Hobbes and Locke, discerned philosophically (not empirically) in the "order of nature" that women are "naturally subordinate to men" (87). Due to man's "superior strength" it is assumed each woman has *always* agreed to "subordinate herself as a wife": that she has agreed to subjugate herself to his will as his property, to obey him in exchange for his protection (86). What she is protected from *includes his own lethal violence*. Specifically, these theorists identify this subordination "reflected in the structure of conjugal relations" exemplified by the marriage contract through which women consent to all ongoing sexual relations, to obey their husbands, sacrifice legal subjecthood, and exist as his property (87). Cott (2002) documents the cultural specificity of marriage used by US post-independence democratic campaigners as a metaphor validating proposed structures for the new government. The social contract, *the archetype of contracts*, and origin story for contemporary democratic politico-legal systems, has consistently relied upon philosophy produced by men structured through the subordination of women as sexual objects – categorically not legal subjects.

The marriage contracts used by these theorists and campaigners have since been moderated. Women in most common law jurisdictions retain independent legal standing after marriage and their property does not immediately transfer to their husband. Technically, rape in marriage is now recognised and women are no longer required to obey their husbands.

However, *the Scene's* contract strongly resembles early marriage contracts. This is particularly tangible in the clause: "*the submissive* shall submit to any activity demanded by *the dominant* and shall do so without hesitation or argument." Noncompliance is punishable with physical violence. Ana rolling her eyes is categorised as "argument"; the punishment is spanking. Further clauses grant Christian control of Ana's diet, exercise, and friendships. *The Scene's* contract imitates both the social contract and historical marriage contracts by confirming a woman's consent to subordination.

Although the cinematic contract resembles BDSM contracts, it differs significantly. A range of safeguards are explicitly designed in BDSM subcultures to reduce abuse (Barker 2013; Tsaros 2013). For example, safe words are often used to communicate the withdrawal of consent during consensual non-consent scenarios (Tsaros 2013, 867; Beres and MacDonald 2015). Participation in BDSM generally involves participants clearly stating their interests and boundaries to aid in finding potential partners. Non-judgemental, honest boundary maintenance and consent practices are prioritised. The theoretical mutuality of BDSM negotiation is absent from *Fifty Shades* in which decisions are predominantly totalising: Christian tells Ana if she does not sign, they cannot have a relationship.

More recent social contract theory shares the gendered assumptions established by the earlier arguments (Pateman 1988, 72). However, these are obscured by de-gendered language and the neutralised individual subject. Thus, although the stories explaining inequality through marriage have largely disappeared, the configuration of gendered differentiation remains, informing contemporary understandings of contract and consent. The social contract sustains "a veneer of equality that masks real and continuing structural inequalities between the sexes" (Drakopoulou 2007, 10). Persistent reliance on contract as something agreed upon by individualised rational actors using their reason continues to exclude women because it requires a degree of abstraction that poorly accommodates many women's experiences (Naffine 2009, 158). Social contract theory continues to exclude women from subjecthood.

Consequently, poststructuralist feminists have argued that the representation of women as subjects in liberal legalism is a dangerous façade (Du Toit 2007; Hunter and Cowan 2007). It encourages a belief that women can unproblematically negotiate contracts, exercise agentic subjecthood, and assert non/consent. Meanwhile, the structural inequality hindering women's subjecthood is hidden. De-gendered language promises the extension of legal subjecthood to women while concurrently denying women's access to that subjecthood by maintaining a particular set of masculine attributes as the base requirement for universal neutrality. Women continue to be philosophically configured as lacking "the capacities to contract" (Pateman 1988, 99). In rape law, while women are presented as able to (not)consent, or perpetrate non-consensual penetration, each woman complainant risks not meeting the criteria for subjecthood. At the heart of the neutrality paradox is a promise that neutrality provides women subjecthood while simultaneously denying women access to subjecthood because *they are not "neutral."*

The same paradox manifests in the suit, and by extension Ana's costume. The uniformity of the suit is an illusion that simultaneously asserts equivalence while it emphasises divergence. For political leadership, the suit symbolises equality through sameness. However, its ill-fit for women's bodies is used as evidence of women's ill-fit for public office. Further, women in corporate attire become grotesque masquerades of masculinity in which femininity is heightened and eroticised. In its resemblance to suits, Ana's dress also promises equality through neutrality while emphasising the very divergences justifying women's inequality.

Subsequently, those who do not fit the uniform or meet subjecthood's criteria are individualised and blamed. Accordingly, Greer's "advice" to Gillard makes Gillard responsible for her "arse" that is "too big" to fit the suit. It also makes Gillard responsible for the discrimination against her as a female prime minister. Rape myths in rape trials hold complainants responsible for penetration they did not want because of clothing choices, alcohol consumption, and friendly behaviour. Correspondingly, employees working in poor conditions are cast as responsible for not negotiating more favourable terms for themselves in individualised contracts. Thus, instead of treating shared patterns of nonalignment with the neutral template as evidence of systemic inequality, discourses of neutrality situate the problem with individual instances of nonalignment. We might call this jurisprudential gaslighting: blaming the victim for the violence perpetrated against them on the basis of their noncompliance with a template designed to exclude them.

The neutrality paradox courses through *the Scene* in the corporate attire, contract language, and *mis-en-scène*. In her sheath dress, Ana does not align with neutrality's specificity. Thus, while the neutrality of *the Scene* appears to grant her the empowerment of subjecthood to negotiate a sexual contract to her advantage, this is deceptive. In a pessimistic poststructuralist feminist interpretation of *the Scene*, the prominence of neutrality ultimately accentuates and eroticises Ana's divergence from liberal subjecthood. Yet at the same time, responsibility for divergence is situated with Ana rather than neutrality's design. Through neutrality discourse, Ana is blamed for failing to meet subjecthood. I will return to this jurisprudential gaslighting below. First, I examine how Ana's ostensibly impenetrably bounded autonomy can be read as ultimately unachievable due to the inherent penetrability of "woman."

Unachievable Autonomy

When Ana steps out of the lift in her sheath dress she appears impenetrable and autonomous. As a protective layer, the sheath reinforces the boundaries of Ana's body: Ana decides who may touch, what her body does and who may penetrate. Impenetrable, isolated boundedness has become a dominant metaphor for autonomy in Western discourses of subjecthood (Nedelsky 1990). Autonomy is a vital promise of liberalism, but it is also another requirement that Ana appears to meet. Yet, as Ana and Christian walk from the lift to the boardroom, a bold zip is exposed running down Ana's back. A zip is an opening. It bears visible and easy access to Ana's body. In a pessimistic poststructuralist feminist interpretation of *the Scene*, the zip is emblematic of Ana's ultimate inability to achieve impenetrable autonomous subjecthood. The zip is sexy, the suggestion of penetrability is sexual, and its metaphorical relationship with autonomy directly relates to rape law jurisprudence.

In historical narratives of the social contract, revolutions broke rigid hierarchies of obligation in which absolute monarchs interfered with the lives and bodies of their subjects. These are stories "about men acquiring mastery over their lives, over their own bodies" (Naffine 1998, 203). Liberalism's emancipation, as a revolution from monarchism, and subsequently as the source of human rights, offers people the capacity to govern themselves, own their own bodies, and act independently of other people and culture. Autonomy as self-mastery and bodily boundedness are core to liberal legalism.

Autonomy is also a recognised principle of rape law jurisprudence across most common law jurisdictions, in international criminal law and human rights discourse (Grewal 2012). This is manifest in the centrality of consent to the definition of rape (Cowan 2007). Non-consensual penetration simultaneously breaches the boundedness of the body and confounds its individualised self-governance, it violates "sexual autonomy and choice" (Cowan 2007, 92). Similarly, employment contracts theoretically enable workers to negotiate what they do with their bodies in exchange for wages, and the health and safety conditions protecting their bodies while they work. Contracts facilitate bodily sovereignty. Consequently, consent-focused rape law relies on the assumption that contracts enable self-regulation of bodily boundaries, and support people to decline offers of penetrative sex. *The Scene's* contract appears to empower Ana to refuse multiple sex acts and limit Christian's control over her. Ana's dress seemingly emphasises the boundedness of her autonomy in its smooth coverage of her body. The integrity of bodily boundaries as a central purpose of law and metaphor for autonomy is discernible in *the Scene*.

Boundaries as metaphors for autonomy have become so powerful that a boundary breach threatens to shatter subjecthood. When a person's "sphere" is penetrated, it is theorised, "the individual is . . . destroyed" (Simmel in Nedelsky 1990, 167). The danger of penetration informs common law's anxieties about anal sex. Between 1603 and 1714, for example, anal penetration attracted a possible death sentence, irrespective of the penetratee's consent (Burg 1981, 70). Later, Blackstone, whose *Commentaries on the Laws of England* (1765–1769) continue to inform legal interpretation, described anal penetration as such a "disgrace to human nature" that its name must not be mentioned by law (Blackstone cited in Raj 2020, 24; Moran 2002). Only in the mid-to-late twentieth century was anal sex decriminalised across most common law jurisdictions. Legal abhorrence of anal sex corresponds with the importance of bodily boundedness and impenetrability to the perceived autonomy of the legal subject.

In a film full of (hetero)sex, the zip down the back of Ana's dress encourages consumers to think of penetrative sex. It provides access through the apparently firm boundary of the sheath – and Ana's autonomy. It is a potential reminder of the persistent structural logics that situate women as incompatible with autonomy's boundedness, because in liberal legalism "women's boundaries seem indistinct" (Nedelsky 1990, 170). Women's bodies leak with menstrual blood, breast milk, and tears, our singularity blurs through pregnancy and culturally gendered patterns of caring. Meanwhile, heteronormativity configures us as always potentially penetrated by sex and inherently vulnerable to non-consensual penetration (Nedelsky 1990, 170; Naffine 2002, 83–84). Women's "corporeal solidness" is rendered a lie (Dworkin in Nedelsky 1990, 170). Ana's zip connotes the ostensibly essential permeability of women's boundaries.

Through the persistent configuration of women as permeable, we are structurally denied subjecthood. Further, the emphasis of law on the penetrative component of *heterosexual* sex – as penile penetration of vaginas – protects men from losing subjecthood when they merge with (female) others during sex (Naffine 2002). Thus, per Dworkin (in Nedelsky 1990, 170), the vagina "appears to be the key to women's lower human status": it is *the* entry point of penetration. The centrality of autonomy *as a bounded body* to legal subjecthood renders penetrative sex a violation – even with consent. Additionally, because women are understood to be susceptible to such violation, as a category we "come to be seen and experienced as something less than fully human" (Nedelsky 1990, 167). Women cannot be legal subjects.

Despite the decriminalisation of anal sex and the de-gendering of rape law, penetration's threat to men's legal subjecthood remains. Graham (2006) argues that when a man identifies as same-sex desiring it is assumed they want to be penetrated. In law's logic, this desire shatters their individual human value. In a rape trial, the logic casts doubt on the "non-heterosexual victim's credibility" (199). Their bounded bodily autonomy is undermined, and the non-heterosexual man is restricted access to full legal subjecthood and justice for sexual violence.

Negation of subjecthood through figurative penetration unfolds like an echo of rape trial cross-examinations in *the Scene* when Christian shares his fantasy of unzipping Ana's dress and "fucking her into next week." This comes after Ana has asserted her agency against his desires by not signing the contract. She confirms his observation that she wants to leave with a declarative "yes." He immediately contradicts her by asserting he reads "something else" in the condition of her body. The press of her thighs, the heat in her cheek, the change of her breathing: all ostensibly "tell" him she wants sex. He reads her body as evidence *against her words*. Christian's authorship of Ana's body repeats a pattern documented across fiction, poetry, and rape trials through which women's refusals are rewritten by men *interpreting* women's bodies "telling them something different." (Larcombe 2005; Philadelphoff-Puren 2005; Naffine 1994). At trial, for example, women's clothes are transformed and read as implied consent by cross-examining barristers: opaque shirts are linguistically rendered diaphanous, swimwear becomes underwear, and leggings turn into stockings (Young 1998). Each alteration sexualises attire, just as Ana's dress transforms from modest corporate attire (sheath) to sexually inviting when the zip is revealed. The sexualised items are then read by men and law as evidence of consent, and women's voices are erased.

Arguing that the structure of erotic love in Western fiction and philosophy is one of male possession and female surrender, Naffine (1994, 13) writes that the figure of a woman "gives herself up to him and he takes her and possesses her." This romantic ideal is also at work throughout legal histories of marriage, inheritance, buggery, and rape. In each instance, women are "implicitly stripped of their sexual agency and subjectivity" (Du Toit 2009, 38). Men's authority, autonomy, and subjecthood are confirmed through their autonomy-obliterating possession of women.

The relational sexing of agency appears to be embedded in English syntax as the act of sex is enunciated: "Man fucks woman: subject verb object" (Mackinnon 1982, 541). Grammatically, the heteronormative formula situates masculine action and feminine passivity as "men *having sex* with women and . . . women *being had*" (Naffine 1998, 211 original emphasis). It is present in the consent-based formula, still haunted by "carnal knowledge" and its unidirectional agency with the woman being known and the man performing the knowing. Heterosex is "a one-sided action done by the man to the body of a woman" (Du Toit 2009, 37).

The Scene's contract has the same agentic structure. The contract was created by Christian and although Ana "negotiates a few terms" she does not propose any herself (Purcell 2013). Further, they remain always "within his framework" (Purcell). Christian initiates: Ana accepts or declines. This extends into their broader relationship such that nothing "in their relationship is hers independently" (Purcell). Explicitly articulated consent is largely absent throughout most of the film. Ana is regularly represented as surprised or shocked by Christian's actions and directions. Further, she is often depicted as uncertain. In the book, this is more explicit, with pages of first-person narration dedicated to Ana's unease. However, as in the romance novels and rape trials analysed by Philadelphoff-Puren (2005), frequent orgasms appear to render the sex consensual. The structure of agency within intimacy in *Fifty Shades* aligns with liberal philosophy in which men's bounded subjecthood is maintained through the breaching of women's autonomy and consequential obliterated subjecthood.

Christian's fantasy is uttered when Ana begins to close the meeting. As such, it appears as a corrective to Ana's asserted agency. Situated within a "business meeting," his fantasy resembles sexual harassment. The spoken imaginary scenario of a man "fucking" a woman on a table at work renders the public (corporate/legal) space pornographic. It grammatically configures a woman as the object of a man's penetrating subjecthood. As part of the spectrum of violence against women, sexual harassment forces each woman's "sense of self into an imaginary space where she is *nothing but* a body, a sex, and a thing to be used and to be acted upon by another" (Du Toit 2008, emphasis original 147). It reminds women that they are "little more than fantasy objects created by and for a world defined by men" (Clark 2005, 125). By articulating his fantasy, Christian potentially shatters Ana's autonomy as a bounded, impenetrable, legal subject in the public realm by reminding us all of her penetrability.

The ubiquity of the sexual violence continuum from rape to sexual harassment means that consumers of women's fiction are often culturally trained to anticipate its injury. Sexual violence has bodily affects prior to and long after an assault (Fileborn and Loney-Howes 2020). Increased heart rates, amplified bodily tension, and physiological arousal activated by *the Scene's* resemblance to familiar moments of unwanted sexual attention are woven through with consumers' understandings of their own agency and capacity to respond to violence – to refuse, denounce, or even enjoy it. Increased physiological tension as anxiety or fear bespeak awareness of vulnerability to violence and the potential impossibility to prevent or redress it. This is an embodied experience of refused autonomy, of knowing one's diminished legal subjecthood. Unachievable female legal subjecthood can be felt throughout the body. The anticipation and response are embodied legal knowledge. And as we might also feel enraged by it, or a mix of titillation and unease, our feelings manifest jurisprudential navigations of il/legitimate behaviour, fairness, autonomy, subjecthood, and justice. The heat of anger flushing our cheeks, righteous opposition clenching our muscles, resistant derision releasing our tension and bursting with laughter – this is jurisprudence of the flesh. I will return to this in my third reading.

A pessimistic poststructuralist feminist legal critique of autonomy as unachievable for women is available in *the Scene*. Ana's zip reminds us

Ana is female and penetrable within her sheath (dress). She does not have control over her body. She is not an autonomous legal subject. The connection between the zip, Ana's femaleness and penetrative sex is strengthened by Christian's fantasy. Although the sex is not realised within *the Scene*, its articulation as fantasy is sufficient to remind consumers of the status of women as objects rather than subjects in its resemblance to sexual harassment. The façade of the protective sheath for Ana's autonomous subjecthood is potentially shattered by the suggestion of penetration. Once again, liberal principles are rendered paradoxical façades by poststructuralist feminism. Ana is read as disempowered by the concept of autonomy because of the liberal legal reliance on the symbolic association between women, penetrative sex, and the shattering of subjecthood. Further still, these façades function to redirect responsibility for failure to fit subjecthood. In the next section, I demonstrate how a poststructuralist feminist reading of *the Scene* identifies jurisprudential gaslighting behind the veneer of Ana's apparent agency.

Agency as Jurisprudential Gaslighting

Ana's refusal to sex and contract in *the Scene* appears to prove her capacity to freely agree, thus establishing her empowered legal subjecthood. Through this veneer of agency, Ana is conferred responsibility for the central relationship, including its ambiguously non/consensual sex. It replicates what poststructuralist feminists have identified nested within liberal legalism's insistence that contracts and consent empower the marginalised: neutrality conspires with autonomy, equality, and agency to present each person as able to (refuse) consent; systemic inequality is then hidden; and the marginalised are rendered culpable for their marginalisation. Through the veneer of agency subordinated people are configured as responsible for the disadvantageous conditions to which contracts (real and imagined) bind them. I'm calling this jurisprudential gaslighting.

The veneer of agency is integral to liberal philosophy from the earliest moments of Social Contract theory. To make sense of entrenched social inequality contract theorists assumed the "only . . . justification for subordination" is consent and that thus each "naturally free and equal individual" must have *agreed* "to be ruled by another" (Pateman 1988, 69). This logic also explained inequality within marriage with a focus on women consenting to subjugation (99). The same veneer strengthens contemporary assumptions that employment contracts enable employees to negotiate better working conditions despite social and economic pressures compelling workers to accept disadvantageous terms. The imaginary existence of the social contract implies that each person *can* exercise their agency when negotiating contracts. Each disadvantageous term is ostensibly due to a weakness of negotiating skill, poor luck or a necessary compromise for another benefit.

Consequently, "much of women's social misery" (pay inequality, discrimination, disproportionate division of household labour, single parenthood, gendered violence) is configured as "consensual" (Drakopoulou 2007, 10). Structural inequalities are presented as women's poor choices or failures to "lean in." For example, women freely *decide* to take maternity leave and care for family, knowing the implications for their careers and financial security when they should *lean in* to professional culture and learn to say "no" (Grant 2013). Women's structural disadvantage is characterised as that to which they each freely agree.

By explaining inequality using contract theory, systemic subjugation is hidden, and the veneer of agency situates responsibility for disadvantage with the subjugated (Pateman 1988). The centralisation of consent in rape law facilitates this gaslighting. A core purpose of rape trials is establishing evidence of (non)consent. Complainants are imagined as empowered by contractual conversations to articulate non-consent. In the absence of consent, complainants are found responsible for making themselves vulnerable by being intoxicated, too friendly, dressed provocatively, or sexually active (Duncanson and Henderson 2014; Ellison and Munro 2009). Hidden behind the assumption of women's agency is law's refusal to recognise women's subjecthood, structural inequalities rendering women vulnerable to sexual violence, and the responsibility of perpetrators for their actions. Ultimately, the consent-focused legal process establishes, again and again, a *truth* that the complainant is responsible for unwanted penetration (Smart 1990).

This jurisprudential gaslighting is enhanced by the promise that gender-neutralising law expands the complainant category. Neutrality conceals the distinct obstacles faced by those who do not "fit" liberal subjecthood and systemic disadvantage is obscured (Ammaturo 2018, 36). Rape complainants are imaginatively removed from their contexts of structural marginalisation. Consequently, responsibility for failure to reach conviction is situated with individual cases rather than further evidence of persistent structural subordination. The complainant is potentially held responsible for both the interpersonal and institutional violence perpetrated against them.

Suits, as the uniform of Western democratic politics, also misdirect culpability for systemic violence. Greer's commentary on Gillard's prime-ministerial suits elides the structural impediments of suit design for women's bodies. Rather, Gillard is judged for not taking responsibility for her own body shape – not "getting over it" and wearing something that fits her "arse." The ill-fit is represented as a woman's fault rather than a consequence of a garment designed for men to enhance their masculine appearance. The conflation of the suit-uniform with public office extends responsibility for discrimination against Gillard as a female national leader to Gillard herself for not "fitting" the role.

Such jurisprudential gaslighting can be read in *the Scene*. By centring the plot upon a contract stipulating the terms of a relationship and its sex, *Fifty*

Shades makes a statement about intimacy as negotiation. The contract provides the most explicit discussion about consent in the film. Ana exercises agency by "striking out" various acts and toys listed in the contract. Her ultimate refusal is dramatic and affective, potentially generating *jouissance* for consumers. The emphatic quality of Ana's refusal proves Ana *can say no* to Christian. Due to *the Scene's* affective drama and its situation in the narrative order, Ana's represented agency makes it possible to read sex throughout the rest of the film as consensual. This effect can be read through a poststructuralist feminist lens as making Ana responsible for the violence perpetrated against her.

The representation of consent to sex is ambiguous throughout most of the film. Explicit contractual conversations are largely absent. Generally, Christian orchestrates the sex and "if Ana doesn't explicitly say 'no,'" it happens (Barker 2013, 898). On occasion, such as described in the book (James 2012, 274), Christian takes Ana by surprise – penetrating without first gaining consent. While Ana "rarely communicates any desires of her own," she is also shown uncomfortable during and following sex: confused, teary, and in pain (Barker 2013, 898). It is possible to read much of the sex as lacking consent – even as causing harm to Ana. However, this is not absolute. The camera angles, music, costuming, editing, and so on encourage romantic reading – directing our attention away from questions about consent towards exchanged gazes between characters and touching bodies. Potential harm is overlaid by orgasms that evidence Ana's enjoyment and imply the sex is not actually harmful. Much of the film's sex is available to be read as masterful seduction or as harmfully non-consensual.

The ambiguity of the represented sex means that its interpretation can be informed by a momentary presentation of Ana's agency. By evidencing that Ana *can say no*, *the Scene* encourages us to believe that she is always able to say no. Thus, in scenes when she neither refuses nor consents, the sex can be read as implicitly consensual. Consequently, her disquiet about the sex becomes her responsibility too: she could have said no but she didn't; she could have walked away, but she didn't. The violence of non-consensual penetration; smacking as "punishment" that leaves Ana unable to sit; Ana's reluctance to refuse various acts for fear of Christian ending the relationship; each become about Ana's indecision and curiosity – her nascent sexuality.

Simultaneously, our attention is redirected from the coercive potential of their differences in age, wealth, social status, and gender. The drama of Ana's refusal in *the Scene*, combined with the romanticisation of her naïve uncertainty about the relationship, masks Ana's structural vulnerabilities with a veneer of agency. While we might enjoy the seduction, the pleasure is not absent of the consensual ambiguity, but the responsibility for the discomforts Ana experiences is situated with Ana.

The centrality of the contract to *the Scene* and the film replicates a pattern poststructuralist feminists have identified at work in liberal legalism, which obscures structural disadvantage while blaming victims for the disadvantage they experience. *The Scene's* presentation of Ana as an agentic contracting subject repeats a pattern of jurisprudential gaslighting through which systemic disadvantage is obfuscated, and the harmed person is held responsible for the harm perpetrated against them. The paradoxes within the promises of neutrality, insistence on autonomy, and assumptions of equality as sameness, that I have mapped in *the Scene* through a poststructuralist feminist interpretation, contribute to this jurisprudential gaslighting. Hence, while *the Scene* can be enjoyed as empowering through a liberal feminist celebration of Ana's subjecthood, it can also be read as disempowering through pessimistic poststructuralist feminist critique.

Theorising Law at the Cinema

This chapter has done two things. The first was to execute a pessimistic poststructuralist feminist legal analysis of *the Scene* from *Fifty Shades of Grey*. Reading in the semiotics of dialogue, plot, movement, editing, costuming and *mise-en-scène* a paradoxical subordination of women's legal subjecthood and simultaneous making women responsible for the sexual violence perpetrated against us. By doing the first I complete a second: demonstrating that more than one theory of law is available in a single scene from cinema. A central purpose of this chapter is to establish that consumers are juggling multiple possible understandings of legal concepts while watching movies. In this way, they are theorising law.

My choice of theories to track through *the Scene* and illustrate my argument is particularly useful for demonstrating the presence of more than one legal theory because of the intimacy between poststructuralist and liberal feminisms. Each critical argument of my poststructuralist analysis is a counterpoint to a liberal feminist hope of accessing legal subjecthood and sexual agency for women. Thus, the liberal promise of neutrality is revealed by poststructuralist feminism as disguising the exclusionary criteria of legal subjecthood, while also situation responsibility for subordination with the bodies that do not conform. I read this as particularly available in the corporate costuming and *mise-en-scène* of *the Scene*. Meanwhile, the metaphor of impenetrable boundedness criteria for autonomous liberal legal subjecthood is particularly exclusionary for women, especially in the epitomising conceptualisation of sexual violence as rape. Ana's dress can be read as illustrating the exclusionary nature of bounded autonomy as a "sheath" dress with an emphatically visible zip drawing attention to Ana's penetrability. The final jurisprudential conflict I identify is Ana's non-consent as agency. My poststructuralist reading rejects my liberal feminist celebration of Ana's refusal to sign the contract and have sex on the table. Instead, my poststructuralist analysis reads *the Scene* as offering a false promise of subjecthood that makes it look like Ana/women have agency. This illusion of agency is then used to blame Ana/

women for the violence perpetrated against them. I suggest that this is jurisprudential gaslighting. Due to poststructuralism's focus on the unveiling of liberalism's paradoxes maintaining the oppressions liberalism promises to overcome, poststructuralism and liberalism are inseparable. Their entanglement is useful for demonstrating that at least two theories of law are available in this single scene from women's fiction.

Each strain of feminism applied so far in this book might be used to interpret *the Scene* in opposition to the other. Yet, one feminist (me, for example) can find validity in both simultaneously. This is because neither feminist approach has achieved stable, agreed-upon, transcendent truths. Rather, both are constantly challenged, reflected upon and theorised differently. But also, because theorist consumers are not static nor are explanations of law. As everyday users of law, we constantly re-evaluate, drift into new ways of understanding, hold persistently dissonant core beliefs, are persuaded by others, . . . and so on. We constantly *become* a little legally different with the laws we brush up against as we move through our social world. Additionally, as users of law, we are continually processing old and new information as we traverse through endless "atmospheres of law" (Philippopoulos-Mihalopoulos 2013). When we are at the cinema, the signifiers are not innately attached to transcendent ideas or narratives. As consumers, we labour to interpret them using our internal semiotic libraries of conflicting cultural knowledges and our variously acculturated sensorium. Consequently, while I present two examples of two feminist legal interpretations of *the Scene*, each consumer's recognition and comprehension of its contract and consent will differ from the consumer sitting beside them in the cinema, each informed by their angle of arrival.

More than one feminist legal theory is available in this brief cinematic moment. Consumers of this much-maligned text of women's fiction are juggling multiple possible interpretations of legal concepts while they watch. This is jurisprudence.

In the next chapters, I demonstrate that this jurisprudence is experienced and practised through the whole of the bodies of these consumers. To usher in this shift in focus I indulge in an autoethnographic reflection on watching another snippet of screen romance which was adapted from web presence and book form, *Heartstopper* (Oseman 2019; Lyn 2022–2023).

Bibliography

Ammaturo, Francesca Romana. (2018). Can Human Rigths Exist without Gender? LGBTQI Issues and the Council of Europe. In Agha, Petr (Ed). *Law, Politics and the Gender Binary* (pp. 33–44). Routledge. https://doi.org/10.4324/9781351047005-4

Barker, Meg. (2013). Consent is a Grey Area? A Comparison of Understandings of Consent in *Fifty Shades of Grey* and on the BDSM Blogosphere, *Sexualities*, 16(8), pp. 896–914.

Beres, Melanie, and MacDonald, Jo. (2015). Talking About Sexual Consent. *Australian Feminist Studies*, 30(86), pp. 418–432.
Blackstone, William. (1826). *Commentaries on the Laws of England, Volume* 2. William Walker.
Boshoff, Anél. (2007). Woman as the Subject of (Family) Law. In Hunter, Rosemary, and Cowan, Sharon (Eds). *Choice and Consent* (pp. 41–57). Routledge-Cavendish.
Burg, B. R. (1981). Ho Hum, Another Work of the Devil: Buggery and Sodomy in Stuart England. *Journal of Homosexuality*, 6(1–2), pp. 69–78.
Clark, Michael J. (2005). Deconstruction, Feminism, and Law: Cornell and MacKinnon on Female Subjectivity and Resistance. *Duke Journal of Gender Law and Policy*, 12, pp. 107–130.
Clemente, Deidre. (November 7, 2016). A President in a Pantsuit? *The Conversation*. https://theconversation.com/a-president-in-a-pantsuit-68286
Clinton, Hilary. (2017). *What Happened*. Simon and Schuster.
Cott, Nancy. (2002). *Public Vows: A History of Marriage and the Nation*. Harvard University Press.
Cowan, Sharon. (2007). Choosing Freely: Theoretically Reframing the Concept of Consent. In Hunter, Rosemary, and Cowan, Sharon (Eds). *Choice and Consent: Feminist Engagements with Law and Subjectivity* (pp. 91–105). Routledge-Cavendish.
Crawford, Lucas. (2009). Refashioning the Architectonics of Gender. *English Studies in Canada*, 35(2–3), pp. 18–20.
Drakopoulou, Maria. (2007). Feminism and Consent: A Genealogical Inquiry. In Hunter, Rosemary, and Cowan, Sharon (Eds). *Choice and Consent: Feminist Engagements with Law and Subjectivity* (pp. 15–44). Routledge-Cavendish.
Du Toit, Louise. (2007). The Conditions of Consent. In Hunter, Rosemary, and Cowan, Sharon (Eds). *Choice and Consent Feminist Engagements with Law and Subjectivity* (pp. 91–106). Routledge-Cavendish.
Du Toit, Louise. (2008). The Contradictions of Consent in Rape Law. *South African Review of Sociology*, 39(1), pp. 140–155.
Du Toit, Louise. (2009). *A Philosophical Investigation of Rape: The Making and Unmaking of the Feminine Self*. Hoboken.
Duncanson, Kirsty. (2014). Truth in Sentencing: The Narration of Judgment in R. v. Webster. In Douglas, Heather, Bartlett, Franchesca, Luker, Trish, and Hunter, Rosemary (Eds). *Australian Feminist Judgments: Righting and Rewriting Law* (pp. 309–316) Hart Publishing.
Duncanson, Kirsty, and Henderson, Emma. (2014). Narrative, Theatre and the Disruptive Potential of Jury Directions in Rape Trials. *Feminist Legal Studies*, 22, pp. 155–174.
Duncanson, Kirsty, and Henderson, Emma. (2022). Interpellation by Design: Could Court Buildings Influence Jury Decision Making. In Duncanson, Kirsty, and Henderson, Emma (Eds). *Court Architecture, Design and Social Justice* (pp. 107–139). Routledge.
Ellison, Louise, and Vanessa Munro. (2009). Reacting to Rape: Exploring Mock Jurors' Assessments of Complianant Credibility. *The British Journal of Criminology*, 49(2), pp. 202–219.

Feinberg, Leslie. (2006). Transgender Liberation: A Movement Whose Time Has Come. In Stryker, Susan, and Whittle, Stephan (Eds). *The Transgender Studies Reader* (pp. 205–220). Taylor and Francis.
Fileborn, Bianca, and Loney-Howes, Rachel. (2020). *#MeToo and the Politics of Social Change*. Palgrave MacMillan.
Freedman, Mia. (August 2, 2010). Critiquing Julia's Clothes is Wearing Thin. *Sydney Morning Herald*. www.smh.com.au/politics/federal/critiquing-julias-clothes-is-wearing-thin-20100802-111pf.html
Goodall, Jane. (April 26, 2013). Dressing the Part: Women, Power, Fashion and that Bloody Jacket. *The Conversation*. https://theconversation.com/dressing-the-part-women-power-fashion-and-that-bloody-jacket-13659
Graham, Ruth. (2006). Male Rape and the Careful Construction of the Male Victim. *Social & Legal Studies*, 15(2), pp. 187–208.
Grant, Melissa Gira. (March 3, 2013). "Like" Feminism. *Jacobin*. www.jacobinmag.com/2013/03/like-feminism/
Grewal, Kristen. (2012). The Protection of Sexual Autonomy Under International Criminal Law: The International Criminal Court and the Challenge of Defining Rape. *Journal of International Criminal Justice*, 10(2), pp. 373–396.
Hollander, Anne. (2016). *Sex and Suits: The Evolution of Modern Dress*. Bloomsbury.
Hunter, Rosemary, and Cowan, Sharon. (2007). *Choice and Consent: Feminist Engagements with Law and Subjectivity*. Routledge-Cavendish.
James, E. L. (2012). Fifty Shades of Grey. Vintage Books.
Kristeva, Julia. (1984). *Revolution in Poetic Language* (Waller, Margaret Trans.). Columbia University Press.
Kristeva, Julia. (2000). *The Sense and Non-Sense of Revolt: The Powers and Limits of Psychoanalysis* (Herman, Jeanine Trans.). Columbia University Press.
Kurzweil, Edith. (2017). *The Age of Structuralism: From Levis-Strauss to Foucault*. Routledge.
Larcombe, Wendy. (2005). *Compelling Engagements: Feminism, Rape Law and Romance Fiction*. The Federation Press.
Larcombe, Wendy. (2011). Falling Rape Convictions: (Some) Feminist Aims and Measures of Rape Law. *Feminist Legal Studies*, 19, pp. 27–45.
Lyn, Euros (Director). (2022–2023). *Heartstopper* [Television] See-Saw Media, Netflix.
Mackinnon, Catharine A. (1982). Feminism, Marxism, Method, and the State: An Agenda for Theory. *Signs: Journal of Women in Culture and Society*, 7(3), pp. 515–544.
Moran, Leslie. (2002). *The Homosexual(ity) of Law*. Routledge.
Munro, Vanessa. (2008). Constructing Consent: Legislating Freedom and Legitimating Constraint in the Expression of Sexual Autonomy. *Akron Law Review*, 41, pp. 923–956.
Naffine, Ngaire. (1994). Possession: Erotic Law and the Law of Rape. *Modern Law Review*, 57, pp. 10–37.
Naffine, Ngaire. (1998). The Legal Structure of Self-Ownership: Or the Self-Possessed Man and the Woman Possessed. *Journal of Law and Society*, 25(2), pp. 193–212.

Naffine, Ngaire. (2002). Can Women be Legal Persons? In James, Susan, and Palmer, Stephanie (Eds). *Visible Women: Essays on Feminist Legal Theory and Political Philosophy* (pp. 69–90). Hart Publishing.
Naffine, Ngaire. (2009). *Law's Meaning of Life: Philosophy, Religion, Darwin and the Legal Person*. Bloomsbury Publishing.
Nedelsky, Jennifer. (1990). Law, Boundaries, and the Bounded Self. *Representations*, 30, pp. 162–189.
Oseman, Alice. (2019). *Heartstopper*. Hatchette Children's Group.
Pandell, Lexi. (November 8, 2016). How Clinton Supporters Made the Pantsuit a Serious Symbol of Power. *Wired*. www.wired.com/2016/11/clinton-pantsuits/
Papadelos, Pam. (2010). *From Revolution to Deconstruction: Exploring Feminist Theory and Practice in Australia*. Peter Lang.
Pateman, Carol. (1988). *The Sexual Contract*. Polity Press.
Philadelphoff-Puren, Nina. (2005). Contextualising Consent: The Problem of Rape and Romance. *Australian Feminist Studies*, 20(46), pp. 31–42.
Philippopoulos-Mihalopoulos, Andreas. (2013). Atmospheres of Law: Senses, Affects, Lawscapes. *Emotion, Space and Society*, 7, pp. 35–44.
Purcell, Carey. (March 4, 2013). Fifty Shades of Feminism – *a Response to E. L. James* [Blog Post]. www.careypurcell.com/articles/8141
Raj, Senthorun. (2020). *Feeling Queer Jurisprudence: Injury, Intimacy, Identity*. Routledge.
Saccardi, Nadia. (2018). Who Wore the Breeches?: An Insight into Early Modern Female Cross-Dressing, Between the 1570s and 1625. *Critical Studies in Men's Fashion*, 5(1–2), pp. 55–70.
Satenstein, Liana. (November, 2016). Wearing the Pantsuit: One Vogue.com Writer Goes Looking for the Hillary Clinton Effect. *Vogue*. www.vogue.com/article/pantsuit-hillary-clinton-effect
Scales, Ann. (2009). Postrstructuralism on Trial. In Albertson Fineman, Martha, Jackson, Jack E., and Romero, Adam P. (Eds). Feminist and Queer Legal Theory: Intimate Encounters, *Uncomfortable Conversations* (pp. 395–410). Routledge.
Sears, Clare. (2015). *Arresting Dress: Cross-Dressing, Law, and* Fascination in Nineteenth-Century San Francisco. Duke University Press.
Smart, Carol. (1990). Law's Power, the Sexed Body, and Feminist Discourse. *Journal of Law and Society*, 17(2), pp. 194–210.
Stacey, Helen. (1996). Legal Discourse and the Feminist Political Economy: Moving Beyond Sameness/Difference. *Australian Feminist Law Journal*, 6(1), pp. 115–134.
Stryker, Susan. (2008). Transgender History, Homonormativity, and Disciplinarity. *Radical History Review*, 100, pp. 145–157.
Sydney Morning Herald. (August 28, 2012). Greer Defends "Fat Arse" PM Comment. www.smh.com.au/politics/federal/greer-defends-fat-arse-pm-comment-20120828-24x5i.html
Taylor-Johnson, Samantha (Director). (2015). *Fifty Shades of Grey* [Film] Focus Features, Michael De Luca Productions, Trigger Street Productions, Universal Pictures.

Tsaros, Angelika. (2013). Consensual Non-Consent: Comparing EL James's *Fifty Shades of Grey* and Pauline Réage's *Story of O*. *Sexualities*, 16(8), pp. 864–879.

Young, Alison. (1998). The Wasteland of the Law, the Wordless Song of the Rape Victim. *Melbourne University Law Review*, 22(2), pp. 442–465.

Interlude – Why am I Crying?

My eyes sting, my nose runs, I feel emotionally wrung out. Trapped in the thrall of more teen romance, I've stayed up to watch *Heartstopper* Episode 3: "Kiss" (Lyn 2022).

"Kiss" has lifted me, dropped me, and caught me on a sensational journey ending in tears. My heart swelled and my skin tingled when the ostensibly straight boy (Nick) invited his boy crush (Charlie) to a party, expressing his vulnerability by stating "I really want you to be there." My buoyancy is sustained by the screenshot of texts between friends articulating value and care for each other with heart emojis and declarations of platonic love. This is warmth and security but also growing nervous excitement as the party approaches.

At the party: romantic expectation, empathic elation and partially realised desire are interwoven with waves of anxiety about homophobic violence, sexual assault and abandonment. As narrative twists, these unfold in quick succession: Charlie finds Nick; Nick leaves Charlie; bullies pressure Nick towards heterosexual performance; Tara tells Nick she is gay; Charlie disappears; Nick calls out the bullies' homophobia; Charlie stands up to his violent ex; a girl confesses her crush on Nick; Nick sees Tara dancing with and kissing her girlfriend; Nick finds Charlie; Nick touches Charlie's hand; Charlie touches Nick's fingers; *Charlie and Nick kiss*; Nick is called away by the bullies; Charlie is alone and uncertain; Nick returns; Charlie is gone.

My heart rate is up, and my skin is alive to the gentlest touch. I am aroused. I am alert and ready to respond in case of the threatened violence presented by the bullies and Charlie's ex. But I am also ready to indulge in the pleasure offered by the dancing, touching, and kissing.

My arousal is fuelled by the rapid succession of narrative moments; the music's strong beat, swells and dissipations; the rainbow light silhouetting Tara and her girlfriend; the shadows shrouding Charlie's ex; Nick spotlighted and still amongst the crowd dancing in slow motion; and the animation inflecting intimate scenes with flowers, autumn leaves and electric charges. My arousal is stirred, enhanced, and sustained by cinematic effects.

DOI: 10.4324/9780429330414-8

CLUNK. A car door closes Charlie into a capsule with his father. There is a pause. Charlie's dad asks, "are you ok?" I break with Charlie. Tears as Charlie turns towards his father whose arms wrap around him. Sobbing as his father says "It's ok, it's ok. I've got you."

My tears are Charlie's, empathising with his confusion and abandonment. These feelings are intensified by the stillness after the party chaos. Both the arms and the words of Charlie's father engulf me and hold me as I drop from hyper-alert, through desertion and into the imagined security of the embrace. But I'm also crying at the fragile hope that my own children might feel that security in my arms when they are teenagers.

This episode moves me; it *affects* me. My body feels the narrative. Even though my conversations with colleagues, Georgia and Matt, prompt cynicism about queer romance created and consumed by straight women and the neutered representation of young gay sexuality. I indulge in the sensations generated between "Kiss" and myself while I simultaneously critique the text and that part of the text that is me (one of those ostensibly straight women consuming domesticated queer romance).

Legal philosophy weaves through my consumption too, distinguishing illegitimate, non-consensual from ethically sought consensual intimacy, adding a sharp sweetness to the swelling satisfaction of Nick and Charlie's kiss. The wrong of discrimination and homophobic violence is made flesh in the cinematically evoked anticipation of the bullies' possible actions. A visceral sense of justice infuses Charlie's triumph over his ex, and relief that sexual violence was not perpetrated. The pleasure – *jouissance?* – generated by the dancing and kissing girls and the boys touching and kissing (representations of same-sex desire) speak to law's definitions of lawful intimacy and too recent debates about marriage law.

This interlude marks a shift in the analysis and argument of this book towards a deeper focus on embodied engagements with cinematic jurisprudence.

Bibliography

Lyn, Euros (Director). (2022). "Kiss". *Heartstopper* [Television] See-Saw Media, Netflix.

Third Reading 1

Legal Sensations between Orgasms

My final reading of *the Scene* from *Fifty Shades of Grey* (Taylor-Johnson 2015) concerns the way jurisprudential practice weaves through the visceral exercise of consuming cinema. This is about cinematic effects generating philosophically and legally by way of stirring reactions in consumer-bodies with signifying sensational textures and ostensibly a-signifying intensities of feeling. While the next chapter returns to consumer agency to demonstrate active phenomenological theorising of legal meaning, this chapter establishes how ideas are communicated and shaped throughout bodies during the consumption of screen-based texts. I begin with a semiotic analysis of "preferred" bodily responses: identifying and interpreting sensations stimulated by cinematic conventions. Particularly noted are legally meaningful *affects*. Cinematic effects are charted as they entice us to *lose ourselves* within *the Scene* – suspend our disbelief and enjoy its jurisprudential offerings with the whole of our bodily selves. *Loss of self* encourages embodied identification. This includes empathic *affective* identification with legal ideas. I read the signification of corporeal responses to *the Scene* to illustrate how phenomenological engagements interpret text, and to discern the resonance of legal philosophy through interactions between body and *Scene*.

I focus on two affective elements of *the Scene*: sound and arousal. *The Scene* is a climactic moment within a film recognised as pornographic romance (McAlister 2015; Boyle 2018). Pornography and romance are "body genres," the conventions of which are designed to stir physical reaction (Williams 1991). Sound and arousal are critical to the bodily qualities of both. While sound involves a range of effects produced to be experienced throughout bodies, arousal is a desired bodily condition sought using effects including sound, but also lighting, editing, shot construction, dialogue, action, . . . and so on. In *the Scene*, sound conspires with other conventional elements to render it romantic rather than violent. Concurrently, the physiological state of arousal is central to the categorisation of *Fifty Shades* as pornographic (Boyle 2018, 86). The affective qualities of sound and arousal help infuse *the Scene* with erotic romance. As such, they also inform the way that the contract and Ana's (non)consent are experienced by consumers. Separately and together, they

DOI: 10.4324/9780429330414-9

shape the ideas generated between consumer and text; they deliver an embodied texture to the legal concepts available; and they influence how those concepts are registered, processed, and enjoyed. My focus on sound and arousal allows me to illustrate how *the Scene's* consumers are invited to experience jurisprudence as bodies at the cinema.

Music, Silence, and the Clatter of Objects on Hard Surfaces

The Scene's soundtrack is surprisingly complicated, with sections of silence between stretches of non-diegetic (incidental or background) music over dialogue. The silences are interrupted by noises from ordinary objects. At the cinema, sound "ceaselessly influences what we see," unendingly influencing our interpretation of moving images and enabling us to perceive more in an image than we would without (Chion 2016, 152). Music, noise, and silence bear information for us to gather and contribute to our sense-making of film. Crucially, the physics of sound reverberates that information through flesh and bone. As vibration, music enables ideas to penetrate our corporeality. In contrast, silence *as the absence of vibration* is also meaningful. Concurrently, sound encourages us to *feel* emotion and noises provide *impressionistic effects*, or notional perceptions and ideas, as well as practical information about objects, movements, and locations. Sound directs our gaze, guiding our ocular focus and our interpretive attention. In a scene about a contract that sets the parameters of sexual play and the composition of an intimate relationship, sound within *the Scene* brings embodied meaning to law.

Listening is fully embodied. The materiality of sound is crucial to the production of meaning at the cinema because it works ideas and narratives into the physiology of individual consumers. Sound weaves us together with text by literally making our viscera vibrate. According to physics, sound is:

> a wave that, following the shaking movement of one or more sources . . . propagates in accordance with very particular laws, . . . touches . . . the ear, where it gives rise to auditory sensations . . . also touching . . . other parts of the body, where it sets off shocks, covibration, and so forth.
>
> (Chion 2016, 16)

Sound resonates across space and through eardrums; reverberates in stomachs; is felt in feet, skin and organs (Young 2016). Experienced in flesh and bone, cartilage and hair follicles, sound is perceived using the whole of our bodies. Through the reverberation of cinematically delivered sound, "as air-bound vibration," into the matter of our bodies, we become connected physiologically with the film we are watching (Donnelly 2005, 13). The physicality of sound *touches* us and thus creates a "bridge" between screen and audience (13). We become part of the text.

Incidental music epitomises ways in which tendrils of sound weave consumers into the philosophy of a cinematic text. Although designed *not* to be noticed, incidental music bears narrative significance and influences how we read the scenes we consume, agitating the matter of our bodies. Creating a sense of atmosphere, incidental music also indicates character mood and suggests emotional responses. Meanwhile, some of its narrative significance is born through its auditory references to previous contexts in which similar phrasings and motifs, beats, rhythms, and melodies have been heard. Film music is a "cogenerator of narrative affect that skews the viewer/listener towards a culturally determined reading of the characters and situations" (Brown 1994, 32). Incidental music helps tell cinematic stories, enriching what we can know about what is on screen, and it does this via air-bound vibrations that resonate through our physical beings.

The tempo of the music behind *the Scene's* initial flirtatious dialogue is *allegro*: fast and bright, or "lively." It sounds like playful violin and xylophone in a modern echo of Mozart. For regular romance consumers, *allegro* piano and strings reminiscent of the classical period (1720–1830) are familiar from previous scenes of benign foolishness and romantic confusion, or trailers for light-hearted period dramas. It connotes frivolity, innocence or playful courtship.

As *the Scene* progresses, the incidental music slows into stretched chords, inciting tension. A strong beat is introduced during Christian's stated sexual fantasy. The music becomes resonant of climactic scenes in thrillers. The build suggests danger. In this instance, the build promises exciting sex. When Ana ends the meeting, the music fades over the sound of her receding heels striking hard floor.

The *allegro* tempo contributes to *the Scene's* sense of excitement, a vibration connecting consumers to the action by stirring excitement in their flesh. Subsequently, consumers' growing desirous anticipation of sexual activity stimulated by the dialogue is compounded by the tension-building music and is then supported by the gentle ebb of the music when the desire is denied by Ana's refusal. Although the music changes when *the Scene* shifts direction, the initial significance of the *allegro* informs how the rest of the scene is interpreted. Consequently, despite the content of the contract listing potentially discomforting controls over Ana's life, consumers are encouraged to read it as playful and romantic. The plotting of flirtation through almost sex and then desire refused is supported by the score. But further than this, the rhythms, beats, chords and tones work the energy of those plot points through the bodies in the cinema. We feel the lightness, building tension and disappointment in part because our organs are vibrating accordingly.

Contrasting the ubiquity of incidental music, silence is uncommon in cinema. Absence of non-diegetic music is "capable of delivering the most powerful musical frisson of all" (Sullivan 2006, xv). Silence as a musical hiatus affects changes in listener awareness. In *the Scene*, the music pauses several times: when Ana is ushered into the boardroom; when she asks about butt plugs; and when Christian declares he "would like to fuck [Ana] into the middle of next week." The affective, disruptive quality of silence draws attention to characters' emotions. For example, the sudden silence when Ana asks about butt plugs mimics the experience of saying something intimate too loudly in a crowded space, just as silence falls. The soundtrack exaggerates the impression of Ana's naivety as embarrassment. At other moments silence contributes to the perception of each character's anticipation of sex.

Within the silences, the sound of stiletto heels on bare floor, paper slipping through an envelope, and pens clattering on a tabletop appear clear and sharp. They are noises often barely registered in everyday life but are emphasised in this scene through film production. Cinematic sound offers considerable information. When sound is voice, we discern from it (not particularly accurately) age, sex, ethnicity, race, health, other physical attributes, and facets of speaker identity. Barthes (1977) calls this "*the grain of the voice*." Similarly, noise informs us of the texture and weight of an object, its position in space, and how full or empty (solid or hollow) it might be. Sound is "materialising" (Chion 2016, 159–160).

Noises in *the Scene* grant substance to the contract equipment, audibly lending weight and thus also gravitas to pen and paper. The noises materialise the unseen "sexy" footwear (stilettos) of all the female characters. In contrast, we don't hear Christian's shoes squeak or clomp. Situated within silence, the sonic clarity of these noises mimics the experience of momentous events, in which one becomes intensely aware of incidental details. Noises as "markers . . . help engender a feeling of breathless expectancy, not unlike the physical sensation of love" (Lehman 2018, 26): in this scene, they replicate conditions of lust and arousal. The idea of "contract" gains dimensions of importance and erotic romance in part through sound production exaggerating awareness of specifically signifying objects associated with contract negotiation and feminised sexuality.

Simultaneously, sound provides *impressionistic effects*. For example, Chion (2016, 158) demonstrates how a whistle "translates as agility": despite not being a realistic sound, consumers perceive the whistle sound to be caused by a visually depicted sword slicing through air. The whistle *gives the impression* of speed, accuracy, and skill (agility) to the sword-wielding character. Correspondingly, the crisp quality of noise within silence can be read in conjunction with *the Scene's* corporate *mise-en-scène*. The space and soundscape are bare; the noises are neither obstructed by soft furnishings, nor diegetic, or incidental music. In architecture, unadorned surfaces denote neutrality – that quality revered in liberal philosophy providing ideal conditions for legal processes such as contract negotiation (Duncanson and Henderson 2022; Henderson and Duncanson 2019).

The juxtaposition of noise and silence provides *impressionistic effects* which contribute to *the Scene's* legal narrative: they connote legal values, provide gravitas to "legal" documents, and overlay legal practices with libidinal charge. Simultaneously, incidental music prompts us to read *the Scene* through an erotically romantic lens. These cinematic effects tickle our senses and vibrate our organs such that even though we may not notice them cognitively, sound is shaping our enjoyment while also informing how we interpret the legal ideas available within the text.

The Function of Arousal

While sound functions as a set of cinematic effects, arousal is a bodily condition pursued using effects. Arousal is awakened bodily alertness and heightened sensory perception. It includes increased heart rates and haptic sensitivity. The term is regularly used to refer to the augmentation of sexual desire. Within a film filled with explicit sex acts, *the Scene's* arousal is sexual. It is all about anticipating sex. Sexual arousal can have an urgency that informs consumption of narrative with a strong determination towards climax. It narrows audience focus and directs interpretation while also seducing us to *be consumed* by sensation. Due to its deeply visceral quality, arousal can also lend naturalness to feelings stirred within its narrative range. Thus, situating a contract negotiation inside a scene involving sexual play potentially renders both the negotiation and the contract *innately* erotic. Sexual arousal saturates all that it touches with erotic significance, including jurisprudence. Before demonstrating how sound and arousal conspire with further cinematic effects to draw consumers to lose themselves in *the Scene* and empathically entangle (identify) with its legal philosophy, I ascertain the relationship between arousal and cinematic signification.

In pornography, arousal is typically partially stimulated through the mimesis by consumer-bodies of screen bodies depicted "caught in the grips of intense sensation" (Williams 1991, 142). Although *Fifty Shades* might fall into the genre of pornography in its regular "spectacular display of . . . sex acts" (Paasonen 2007, 46), *the Scene* is less explicitly pornographic. There is a distinct absence of bodies involuntarily convulsing with sexual rapture. Despite this, the scene remains all about sexual arousal for both characters and consumers. This is because it is strewn with signifiers of sex: the naming of sex toys and acts; extreme close-ups of open mouths and pencil nibbling; hands working potential binds; the memory of a zip running from nape to hem; the sound of stilettos against hard floors; and verbally described states of desire. The gratuity of these signifiers is intensified by their context within a movie abundant with explicit sex scenes and the tantalising promise that there *might* be sex *in this scene*.

Although arousal may be stirred using a semiotics of "sex," it is also engendered through more fleeting and less conventionally discernible signifiers. Pornography uses a range of logics and effects that do not "fully translate into semantic models of explanation" (Paasonen 2007, 46). Simultaneously, the effects can be fleeting, and ostensibly random intensities of feeling or *shimmers* can seem to confound "the net that tries to capture meaning" (Steinbock 2019, 145). Ideas and narratives generated by consumers responding to less formulaic effects of cinema are difficult to trace because neither conforms to hegemonic discourse.

Meanwhile, states of arousal shape consumer engagement. Western narrative practices work with an energy that pushes consumers towards resolution. Narrative drive towards climax is amplified in pornography due to the alignment of sparse plots and phallic determination towards orgasm (Johnson 1993). Conventionally, sexual arousal appears to augment urgency to arrive at a particular conclusion. In this manner, arousal directs consumer focus towards the pornographic components of a text. Simultaneously it eroticises elements not otherwise necessarily arousing – recoding signs with erotic significance through an urgent interpretation of available information towards a gratifying climax. Gaps of logic or non-compliant signifiers can be ignored. In *the Scene*, the erotic drive supports consumers to ignore discomforts about the controlling terms of the contract and invest in Christian's rewriting of Ana's refusal to sex. Further, the contract and Christian's persistence are potentially rendered sexy rather than dangerous, adding to the enjoyment of hetero-masculine violence rather than disrupting it.

However, *the Scene* is less driven to orgasm-as-climax. Arousal is regularly more diffuse than the phallic pursuit of orgasm as ejaculation. In *the Scene*, arousal is more oriented towards prolonged sexual enjoyment and delayed gratification. Consequently, there is a delicious tension between the drive to orgasm and *the Scene's* abrupt end without. Thus, although *the Scene* remains fuelled by sexual urgency, Ana's refusal to sign or have sex heightens audience desire. Her agency and subjecthood are erotically charged.

While a semiotics of sex stimulates arousal for *the Scene* consumers, such enjoyment influences interpretation of its further signifiers, including those connoting law. Hence, contracts become accoutrements for sexual play. Similarly, contract negotiation is rendered sexually exciting. Concurrently, the urgency of arousal compels consumers to focus on embodied desires for climax and to disregard details that diverge. This climax-orientated embodied enjoyment would appear to support a masculinist reading of contract and consent, encouraging consumers to invest in Christian's overwriting of Ana's refusal by reading desire in her body. However, simultaneously Ana's resistance and definitive refusal potentially move consumers past Christian's claim and towards a possibility of even more enjoyable extended and undulating arousal by delaying full gratification. Contract negotiation provides a joyous undulation in the trajectory towards a possibly more satisfying climax down the track. Thus, asserting non-consent is made deliciously possible and even exceedingly sexy.

The Scene's soundtrack contributes to audience arousal, building it and cushioning the denial of its fulfilment. Its music, noise, and silence contribute to the eroticisation of contract and consent, informing legal interpretation. A significant part of the way that sound and arousal shape readings of *the Scene* is by encouraging consumers to become immersed. Consumers are invited to give themselves up to *the Scene*, to become engrossed, and in this way identify deeply through embodied empathy with its ideas and philosophies.

Losing Yourself at the Cinema

Consuming films at the cinema can be absorbing. In the darkened theatre, enormous images augmented by surround sound lure us into dream-like states, fully immersing us in story and aesthetics (Metz 1976). Sound and sexual arousal encourage consumers to enjoy *the Scene* through a *loss of self* – merging with the text with an enjoyment resembling heightened sexual pleasure or *jouissance*. Sound supports consumers to revel in cinematic reality with the whole of their bodies; while arousal intensifies enthrallment by offering physical stimulation and drawing consumers towards cognitive and physiological climax. Barthes' (1977) theorising of *jouissance* and *loss of self* helps to consider the extent to which consumers might suspend their disbelief, quiet their critical analysis, and entertain a film's philosophy with their bodies.

The term *jouissance* means enjoyment both of pleasure and entitlements (rights and property ownership). But it also means sexual pleasure and, particularly, orgasm. Feminine *jouissance* contains something that is "outside the boundaries of the phallus": it is a "different order of pleasure to that of male pleasure" (Brook 1997, 72). Less climax-oriented than the ejaculatory masculine orgasm, feminine jouissance is "without concern about ends or closure": multiple, protracted, ongoing (Marks and Courtivron in Brook 1997, 72). While for Cixous, *jouissance* grants access to women's creativity, for Kristeva it is that which pre-exists the imposition of patriarchal culture and persists as a marginalised excess eluding dominant structures. In cultural studies, *jouissance* is the "creative and pleasurable eruption of cultural 'difference' at the 'seams' of the text" (Bordo in Brook 1997, 156). It is rapturous marginalised excess expressing counter knowledges and experiences that cannot be fully contained by the dominant order. It includes phenomenological knowledge and theory which can defy translation into the hegemonic. Above all, *jouissance* is experiential, felt in the body – a physiological conduit of knowledge and philosophy.

Barthes (1977) describes a *jouissance* brought about by listening to music. Immersion in sound "penetrates" the boundaries of the "self," momentarily dissolving the ostensible coherence of individuated subjecthood. The ideal individual of liberal legal philosophy is defied. Musically induced *jouissance* resembles the pleasure of sexual stimulation. *Jouissance* as orgasm is potentially the ultimate "loss of self": *la petite mort* (little death). Orgasm "risks the shattering of the self and identities" (Parreñas Shimizu 17). In a less phallocentric understanding of sexual pleasure, sex can generate a sustained blurring of individuated boundaries in extended feminine *jouissance* – without concern for closure. Brought on through deep engagement with a text, *jouissance* as a *loss of self* involves a dissolving of liberalism's bounded individual and potentially opens consumers to significantly different philosophies from their own.

Arousal in pornography promises direct and rapid loss of self through orgasm. Snitow (in Paasonen 2018, 138) observed a parallel sensual energy of building anticipation towards orgasm across pornography (with orgasm) and romance (without), both leading to the "explosion of the boundaries of the self." However, we could read romance with its explosion of boundaries *without* orgasm as a "feminine" manifestation of *jouissance*: less focused on a singular climax. Pornographic orgasm in *the Scene* appears limited because the sex does not get beyond talking or touching objects. However, as fans of women's fiction, presumed *Fifty Shades* consumers might be caught in a sensational journey driving towards pornographic orgasm while simultaneously enjoying the endless romantic pleasures of delayed gratification and prolonged arousal. *The Scene* provides a beat in a film depicting multiple orgasms generating a sustained state of arousal that supports the blurring of selfhood – perhaps even a creative feminine *jouissance*.

Sound plays an important role in the *loss of self* by supporting consumers to immerse themselves more deeply, sensually, and cognitively in a text. Practically, incidental music maintains audience focus by blocking distracting noise from within and without the theatre. It fills empty spaces in the theatre off-screen and narrative gaps on-screen by swathing audiences in audio sensation (Donnelly 2005; Garwood 2000). Carefully produced soundtracks hold our attention by stimulating as much of our embodied sensorium as cinematically possible. By keeping us focused and reverberating through our senses, film soundtracks encourage us to rest our mental load. Like Radway's (1984, 72) romance novels, cinema sound enables consumers to "deny temporarily the demands" of daily life.

I propose that part of what is "lost" or subdued in the *loss of self* can be the critical self. While allowing ourselves to be swept away with consuming sensation, we are summoned to rest our critical faculties and entertain whatever fictional logic is offered. However, first, it is useful to recognise the capacity of film to seduce us into losing ourselves and allow us to suspend our disbelief. I will go on to how the loss of critical self is never fully complete in the next chapter, but rather that there can be a delicious interplay between letting go of critique while also being able to access that critical self at any moment in order to practice some pleasurable critique.

Incidental music facilitates suspended disbelief by vibrating flesh with mood-effecting beats, cadences, and melodies. Playful rhythms, tense violins, and solid beats in *the Scene* urge acquiescence to a specific range of moods. The music discourages resistance to aberrations of narrative logic or uncomfortable, even otherwise untenable content. Buoyed by the *allegro* melody of innocent romance, consumers are encouraged to enjoy the *Fifty Shades* contract as amorous rather than controlling. To read the terms of the contract extracted from the cinematic context potentially triggers arousal as alertness to systemic violence for some. However, by stimulating pleasurable responses, the music potentially overrides alternative bodily reactions. Instead, the music encodes our sensations as erotic romance. As cinema consumers engrossed in the audio-visual text, we are encouraged to suspend our disbelief about the legitimacy of the represented relationship and the validity of the contract to enjoy the *intensities of feeling* mimicking sensations of love and desire.

Sexual arousal similarly encourages consumers to quiet their discomfort about the contract and Christian's violence. Throughout *Fifty Shades* there is a pattern in which Ana expresses concern about Christian's behaviour and uncertainty about the sex he initiates. However, each time she overcomes her concerns when she achieves orgasm. This echoes rape myths that read consent retrospectively in orgasms or other ostensible indicators of sexual pleasure. Correspondingly, *Fifty Shades* consumers are encouraged to experience their "social constraints . . . overwhelmed by a flood of sexual energy" (Snitow in Paasonen 2018, 138). Thus, as our bodies mimic the arousal described in Christian's reading of Ana's body, we are pushed to ignore unease. Arousal encourages us to find Christian's interpretation more compelling than Ana's own articulated refusal. We are being drawn towards climax. Accordingly, we are supported to relinquish feminist critique, lose ourselves to sensation, and enjoy the promise of non-consensual penetration. Our enjoyment rewards our *loss of self* and justifies our collusion with Christian's violence.

I am identifying multiple affective trajectories in *the Scene*; potentially pulling consumers in different embodied ideological directions simultaneously. No ideological trajectory is truer than another. Rather, they conspire, nourishing each other by contributing to sensational density. Thus, for example, drive towards phallic climax is augmented by Ana's triumphant resistance and any unease about resemblances to sexual violence. Concurrently, phallic drive is integral to a feminine *jouissance* experiencing Ana's triumphant refusal as a (delicious) punctuation point of multiple climaxes in a journey of protracted arousal. The pleasure of delayed gratification involves regular builds towards climax that then decrease before building again to greater and more fulfilling (boundary-breaching, self-exploding) orgasm.

Consequently, the *jurisprudential pleasure* of Ana's refusal to contract and sex can include sensually experienced recognition of coercive violence. It can also encompass simultaneous discomfort with the violence. Enjoyment of discomforting pleasure builds into climactic triumph and simultaneously refused satisfaction which enables delayed gratification. Thus, philosophies of contract and consent concerning sex are informed by arousal. They are woven into a *loss of self* at the cinema. Simultaneously, the sensual experience of sound and arousal encourages a *loss of self* during *the Scene* that informs the way consumers interpret the legal ideas present within it.

Embodied Identification

When the boundaries of individuated selfhood explode or diminish through *loss of self*, identification as visceral empathy becomes possible and embodied empathic identification entangles consumers with the ideas available in a text. In *the Scene*, sound and arousal conspire to empathically align consumers with both Ana and Christian through their bodies while also identifying sensually with *the Scene's* theories of law. I draw together the *loss of self* with Barthes' *grain of the voice* and Steinbock's *shimmers* to demonstrate how sound and arousal facilitate embodied identification with characters and ideas. The depth of cinematic identification available in *the Scene* involves corporeal entanglement with philosophy, including that pertaining to law (jurisprudence).

Loss of self through immersion in music can include imaginary merging with the creator of sound (Barthes 1977). As they lose themselves, listeners can become open to the possibility of empathy with another who might be radically different from themselves (Young 2016, 32). When a listener's coherent sense of singular identity and subjecthood diminishes, they are granted a capacity to understand the experience of another person through that person's frame of reference. Because music is created by a musician's whole body and resonates throughout the listener's body, the empathy experienced is corporeal.

Empathetic embodied identification might be the phenomenological imagining of physically creating the *grain of the voice* (Barthes 1977). The "grain" is the audio-signifier of a singer's age, gender, race, health, and more: what gives the voice texture. Listeners perform the *grain* when they imitate holding power notes, rasping husky depths, and non-lyrical moans with singers while they listen. But physical empathy is also strumming an air guitar, mimicking a drum solo, replicating a vocalist's hair flick or pelvis thrust. Or it is the ghostly sensation of performing these acts, while not actually performing them. Feeling the *grain* resonates for me along the lines of Sobchack (2004), MacDougall (2006), and Ott's (2010) embodied experiencing of cinematically represented movement.

Incidental music is diffuse, without a visible point of origin. Consequently, instead of eliciting imaginative merging with a musician, it can expedite identification with characters. Its physical resonance creates mood and sensation that attach to characters within a scene. This is more obvious when we listen with a character to diegetic music, like Max in *Stranger Things* season 4, episode 1, listening to Kate Bush on her Walkman (The Duffer Brothers 2016-ongoing). We listen with her while we gaze from her point of view at the world through which she is travelling. Dolly shots intercut to focus on her face and body in motion and the music helps us to feel anguish with her.

Within *the Scene*, the *allegro* tempo of the initial music helps consumers feel the flirtatious excitement between Ana and Christian. Then Ana's embarrassed naivety is *felt* dramatically due to the sudden silence. Perceiving a drop in incidental music is physiological, and when felt, identification with Ana is strengthened: *we feel as she feels*. When the violins build and the beat hardens, consumers are prompted to align with Ana and Christian simultaneously: we are all thinking about sex on the table where Ana laid her hand. When Christian describes the signs of Ana's desire, the music encourages us to feel our own legs press together and our own cheeks flushing – feeling her arousal and his. The final tense beats in the scene are not only the sensation of Ana's triumphant refusal but they also embody Christian's unmet desire. However, the abruptness of her refusal is potentially softened by dissolving music. The omnipresence of *incidental* music untethered from diegetic location lends the consumer sensations and stimulates a fluidity of identification. In this way, music facilitates simultaneous, multiple identification, assisting us to feel embodied empathy for both Ana and Christian at the same time.

When listeners' bodies resonate with sound made by another and screen consumers feel the movements they observe, a kinaesthetic relation is generated. "Kinaesthetic" refers to the sensory perception of our bodies' position and movement. When listening to song, consumers hear another's voice *with* and *in relation to* their bodies. They may feel – even perform – the physicality of sound creation. So too do screen consumers comprehend another person's movement *with* and *in relation* to their own bodies. Consumer-bodies imaginatively experience the performing, productive bodies of others – imagine what it feels like to make *that* sound or move *that* way. Feeling *the grain of the voice* involves a powerful range of *affects* that work beyond linguistic or visual semiotics, enabling understanding or connection with the experience and feelings of another. This openness to experience from another's frame of reference is facilitated by enjoyment as *loss of self* through which attachment to one's coherent self is reduced.

Identification in cinema theory has predominantly focused on the visual through Mulvey's (2006) *male gaze. The gaze* is what we can see and how we can see it. It is controlled by *the apparatus*: the camera and all the production of what ends up on the screen. Conventions of Western cinema align *the gaze* with male characters, filming from hetero masculine "points of view." This *male gaze* is epitomised by the way the apparatus makes consumers *look at* the bodies of women characters: lingering over and compartmentalising breasts, hips, lips, and bottoms. Even though what consumers see is controlled, alignment with the camera and key male characters encourages us to feel we *are* in control. By looking with a character, consumers are literally made to see from that character's perspective and consequently identify with them. Mulvey demonstrated that through watching conventionally produced cinema, women learn to look the way men look. Thus, at the cinema, women "cross-identify": women are coerced into the patriarchal system of identifying with heterosexual men objectifying women.

Mainstream pornography exemplifies the male gaze. Johnson (1993) describes pornography as a "genre symbolically dominated by the phallus."

As an industry, pornography has significantly depended upon the "creation of a group of people as commodities for the sexual pleasure of others: a process which is profoundly gendered in its dominant form" (Boyle 2018, 87). Mainstream pornography is predominantly made by men, for heterosexual men in ways that present women as objects for male gratification. Consequently, the genre's "erotic organisation of visibility" (its *gaze*) struggles to envision "women's pleasure beyond phallocentric regimes of representation" (Johnson 1993, 37). The dominance of the *male gaze* makes it difficult to represent women's sexual pleasure or support identification with women characters and experiences.

Cinema theory has since extended our understanding of identification beyond the male gaze. For example, Clover (1992) revealed that young men's identification with female "victim" characters is integral to the joys of horror movies and Young (1997) demonstrated a double identification at work in serial killer films that heightens enjoyment by compelling consumers to see with both victim and killer simultaneously. The pleasure of these genres reaches beyond the hetero-masculine convention of the male gaze, both relying on and aiding identification across gender binaries and with more than one character at once. Cinema conventions are also complicating and diversifying structures of identification. There are subtle alterations in the way gendered characters are presented on screen. In *Fifty Shades*, for example, the cinematic gaze intermittently luxuriates in Christian's body, lingering over shirtless musculature exposed by low-slung jeans. Although it remains an objectifying gaze – about desiring a body and evaluating it in terms of wanting to fuck it – the power of such shots is not situated with a male character. Instead, they follow the lines of Ana's desire and encourage erotic identification with Ana.

Steinbock (2019, 4) argues that cinematic cross-identification "is less uncommon, possibly open to anyone." Building on Barthes' *shimmers*, Steinbock demonstrates multiplicities of identification are achievable. These are the shimmers introduced in my *Introduction*: momentary twinklings of light, snippets of dialogue, fleeting aspects of characters, intensities of feeling and sensation, constantly changing images and the "flickering of frames . . . or of pixels" that constitute cinema (8). Multiplicities are available in shimmers because of their nuance – bearing minuscule gradations of difference; their fleeting evasiveness such that no one can grasp them all; and because they are not only visible but can be experienced as sensation. Thus, although there are dominant structures of heteronormative identification sustained through cinema conventions, shimmers "render available more . . . possibilities of threshold embodiments" and social identities (4). Divergent identification, empathetic, and kinaesthetic connections are available through the manifold fleeting nuances of cinema to be taken up by the diversity of consumers in the theatre.

Being able to grasp individual shimmering trajectories, and the meaning generated with them, depends upon the angle from which each consumer enters the cinema space; consumers cultural training in visual representation and their "subjectively felt lives," acculturated sensorium (Sobchack 2004, 63) or *experienced* bodies (Ott 2010). While the flickering light of a screen-based text refracts with many possible opportunities for consumer identification, not all opportunities are discernible to all consumers but rely upon the unique cultural training of each. Consumers seek and enjoy opportunities to identify with refracting representations that align with different parts of themselves and others with whom they are allied or of whom they have awareness. *Shimmering* identification is far more complex than the "strict male or female grammar" of the male gaze (Steinbock 2019, 4).

Pornography is a compelling site of complex embodied identification. Through its overt pursuit of sexual arousal, porn can provide access to multifarious cross-identification as deep empathic understanding from another's frame of reference. Correspondingly, sexual fantasy often "involves a 'de-subjectification', a varying of subject position so that the subject takes up more than one position" (Keesey 2010, 102). This might be understood using *jouissance* and *loss of self*: when the boundaries of coherent individualised self-identity or subjecthood explode through sexual pleasure, the capacity to feel empathetically is enriched. Porn consumers are not limited by alignment with gender, sexuality or politics "to identification with certain characters" (Ryberg 2015). They are able to cross-identify. Further, consumers may be aroused while viewing acts they would not enjoy "in real life" (Ryberg 2015). Further again, viewer sensations are not necessarily due to engagement with specific characters, but "can be generated by far more random and fleeting encounters with scenes, genres, and characters, even music and dialogue" (Paasonen 2007, 46). Patterns of identification and points of empathy extend beyond human characters to so many other components making up pornographic texts. Williams (1993, 56) notes "how easy" it is to "identify with diverse subject positions and to desire diverse objects" in pornography. Objects become fetishised; ideas gain libidinal charge. As an episode of prolonged *feminine jouissance, the Scene* offers consumers *shimmering* possibilities of multiple, cross-identification, charging legal concepts with erotic energy.

Pornographic *loss of self* and cross-identification can facilitate *affective* identity exploration. Pendleton's (1992) study of male homosexual porn consumption in the 1980s is helpful for thinking about this. While homosexuality was being slowly decriminalised across the common law world, a "main source of representation of male homosexuality" was gay pornography (Pendleton 1992, 155). As such, it enabled many men to "acknowledge and talk about their desire" and try on "different positions, fantasies, kinks" (155–156). Identification with pornography provided opportunities for men to explore different forms of gender and sexuality. Relatedly, identification with masochistic erotica has helped readers explore "how sex can feel, how it works on the body" (Smith in Paasenon 2014, 144). Consumers can try out various "versions of self-in-society" to imagine "what [they] might or might not be" (Barker in Paasenon 2014, 144). This opens "bodily horizons of possibility" through which consumers can visit "distant realms": exploring ideas and ways of being, that they may not have considered before (Paasonen 2018). Such "imaginative play" (Williams 1999, 324) is experienced through the body of the consumer, much like the body memory of acculturated sensoriums and *experienced* bodies in MacDougall (2006), Sobchack (1992), and Ott (2010). Consuming pornography can facilitate empathic identification with a range of subject positions in a manner that involves the whole body of each consumer.

Correspondingly, *Fifty Shades* has been credited with broadening straight women's sexual horizons through the imaginary play of pornographic romance (Jones and Mills 2014). Conservative religious and secular women have been documented using *Fifty Shades* to talk about sex and sexuality (Whitehead 2013; Jones and Mills 2014, 241). The influence of the phenomenon on "straight women's identity formation" is potentially realised in increased sex toy sales (Jones and Mills 2014, 241). Through *jouissance, loss of self*, and embodied identification with the film, consumers of *Fifty Shades* are supported to explore sex in ways not so readily available in much mainstream cinema.

The film provides opportunities to "try on" sexuality differently. The available fantasies are entangled with various understandings of sex and gender, but also of law. Within *the Scene*, these include (but are not limited to) resistance to heteronormative contracts; workplace sexual harassment; masculine overwriting of women's non-consent; and maintaining bodily integrity during sex. Ana's refusal to consent and contract can be felt by consumers as though it is their own delicious triumph against a controlling but alluring man. There is also potential to identify simultaneously with Christian in a way that enjoys the hope sex *will* happen despite Ana's refusal. Consumers may entertain both fantasies and more, identifying with Ana and Christian in different ways, and with the atmosphere of *the Scene*, to generate rich and gratifying pleasure. By imaginatively playing through these fantasies consumers are also sensually engaging with theories of law.

Feeling Jurisprudence

The affective qualities of cinematic texts bear in them potential interpretations of law that are experienced phenomenologically by consumers. In the examples of sound and arousal in *the Scene*, each holds a range of signification, relying on pre-existing semiotics of sensation that attach meaning to the text through effects felt in consumer-bodies. However, sound and arousal also contribute to a state of being akin to ecstasy or sexual pleasure: *jouissance*. Integral to this pleasure is *loss of self* and letting go of a static inherent identity. I argue that this enables a quieting of the critical self, such that the consumer might suspend their disbelief regarding textual inconsistencies. The consumer can thus merge with the text, and fully entertain its logic and arguments. *Jouissance* shatters the boundaries of the self so that the consumer is open to empathising with another who might be significantly different from themselves. Sound and arousal encourage and enable consumers to explore another's experiences and perspectives. While this empathic identification is supported by intensities of feeling, these intensities also bring meaning to the identification, helping consumers to feel what their object of identification might feel phenomenologically. Hence, the perspective of the character or object identified with is woven into consumers' cinematic experience – they feel the ideology of their character/object through their bones and organs. When in *the Scene* consumers affectively and empathically identify with Ana and Christian, they are open to the characters' experiences and perspectives of contract and consent. Consumers are granted access to the characters' embodied knowledges of these legal tools and concepts. In this manner, consumers of *the Scene* are engaged to explore interpretations of law with their bodies.

While embodied engagements with *the Scene* concern the terms of the central couple's relationship and the sex they might (not) have, it also pertains to law as it relates to intimacy. Previously I described the way arousal offers exploration of contract and consent as enabling women legal subjecthood and agency: being heard when negotiating contract terms and asserting agency by refusing consent. This liberal feminist legal philosophy can be felt as exciting and triumphant in *the Scene*. Simultaneously, embodied identification with Christian is also available as the music, images, and dialogue allow consumers to share his arousal, anticipation, and disappointment. Encouraged to want sex as Christian describes it and support his rewriting of Ana's non-consent in pursuit of phallic climax, consumers are offered another interpretation of law. Through embodied identification with Christian, we can explore contract as a means of gaining certainty through ongoing (nonretractable) consent (a rape myth that wields considerable significant power in sexual offence trials); contract and consent as granting authority to perform what otherwise might be criminal harm; and understanding consent as something a man might read in a woman's body against the words she articulates. This is a hetero-masculinist understanding of the law that pervades sexual offence trials. In the jarring between these two perspectives, a pessimistic poststructuralist feminist interpretation might manifest in consumer-bodies, resistant to the draw of character-based identification within *the Scene* but clinging to *shimmers* of identification possible in refracted representations of sexual violence. Through embodied empathic identification, consumers of *the Scene* are engaged in legal interpretation. This is to *experience* embodied jurisprudence at the cinema.

In the next chapter I return to the consumer agency explored in the *Reader Agency* to demonstrate that consumers are actively grappling with these multiple possible interpretations of law with the whole of their bodies – *as* knowing and thinking (theorising) bodies. I draw together the phenomenological experience of cinematic legal theory identified previously with evidence of consumers physically and agentically interacting with their texts to argue that consumers of *the Scene* in *Fifty Shades* are *performing* embodied jurisprudence.

Bibliography

Barthes, Roland. (1977). *Image, Music, Text* (Stephen Heath, Trans). Noonday Press.

Boyle, Karen. (2018). The Implications of Pornification: Pornography, the Mainstream and False Equivalences. In Lombard, Nancy (Ed). *The Routledge Handbook of Gender and Violence* (1st ed., pp. 85–96). Routledge.

Brook, Ann. (1997). *Postfeminisms: Feminism,* Cultural Theory and Cultural Forms. Routledge.

Brown, Mary Ellen. (1994). *Soap Opera and Women's Talk: The Pleasure of Resistance*. Sage.

Chion, Michel. (2016). *Sound: An Acoulogical Treatise* (Steintrager, James A. Trans.). Duke University Press.

Clover, Carol J. (1992). *Men, Women, and* Chain Saws: Gender in the Modern Horror Film. Princeton University Press.

Donnelly, Kevin. (2005). *The Spectre of Sound: Music in Film and Television*. British Film Institute.

The Duffer Brothers (Producers). (2016-ongoing). *Stranger Things* [Television] USA: Netflix.

Duncanson, Kirsty, and Henderson, Emma. (2022). Interpellation by Design: Could Court Buildings Influence Jury Decision Making. In Duncanson, Kirsty, and Henderson, Emma (Eds). *Court Architecture, Design and Social Justice* (pp. 107–139). Routledge.

Garwood, Ian. (2000). Must You Remember This?: Orchestrating the 'Standard' Pop Song in *Sleepless in Seattle*. *Screen*, 41(3), pp. 282–298.

Henderson, Emma, and Duncanson, Kirsty. (2019). Design and Ideology – Innovation in the Magistrates' Court. *Griffith Law Review*, 27(2), pp. 207–232.

Johnson, Eithne. (1993). Excess and Ecstasy: Constructing Female Pleasure in Porn Movies. *Velvet Light Trap*, 31, pp. 30–50.

Jones, Lucy, and Mills, Sara. (2014). Analysing Agency: Reader Responses to *Fifty Shades of Grey*. *Gender and Language*, 8(2), pp. 225–244.

Keesey, Douglas. (2010). Split Identification: Representations of Rape in Gaspar Noé's Irréversible and Catherine Breillat's A ma sœur!/Fat Girl. *Studies in European Cinema*, 7(2), pp. 95–107.

Lehman, Frank. (2018). *Hollywood Harmony: Musical Wonder and the Sound of Cinema*. Oxford University Press.
MacDougall, David. (2006). *The Corporeal Image: Film, Ethnography and the Senses*. Princeton University Press.
McAlister, Jodi. (2015). Breaking the Hard Limits: Romance, Pornography, and the Question of Genre in the Fifty Shades Trilogy. *Analyses/Rerearings/Theories (A/R/T)* Journal, 3(2), pp. 23–33.
Metz, Christian. (1976). The Fiction Film and Its Spectator: A Metapsychological Study. (Guzzetti, Alfred Trans.). *New Literary History*, 8(1), pp. 75–105.
Mulvey, Laura. (2006). Visual Pleasure and Narrative Cinema. In Merck, Mandy (Ed). *The Sexual Subject: Screen Reader in Sexuality* (pp. 22–34). Routledge.
Ott, Brian. (2010). The Visceral Politics of *V for Vendetta*: On Political Affect in Cinema. *Critical Studies in Media Communication*, 27(1), pp. 39–54.
Paasonen, Susanna. (2007). Strange Bedfellows: Pornography, Affect and Feminist Reading. *Feminist Theory*, 8(1), pp. 43–57.
Paasonen, Susanna. (2014). Things to do with the Alternative: Fragmentation and Distinction in Online Porn. In Maina, Giovanna, Biasin, Enrico, and Zecca, Federico (Eds). *Porn After Porn: Contemporary Alternative Pornographies* (pp. 21–36). Mimesis Books.
Paasonen, Susanna. (2018). Many Splendored Things: Sexuality, Playfulness and Play. *Sexualities*, 21(4), pp. 537–551.
Pendleton, David. (1992). Obscene Allegories: Narrative, Representation, Pornography. *Discourse*, 15(1), pp. 154–168.
Radway, Janice A. (1984). *Reading the Romance: Women, Patriarchy, and Popular Literature*. University of North Carolina Press.
Ryberg, Ingrid. (2015). Carnal Fantasizing: Embodied Spectatorship of Queer, Feminist and Lesbian Pornography. *Porn Studies*, 2(2–3), pp. 161–173.
Sobchack, Vivian. (2004). *Carnal Thoughts: Embodiment and Moving Image Culture*. University of California Press.
Sobchack, Vivian Carol. (1992). *The Address of the Eye: A Phenomenology of Film Experience*. Princeton University Press.
Steinbock, Eliza. (2019). Shimmering Images: Trans Cinema, *Embodiment, and the Aesthetics of Change*. Duke University Press.
Sullivan, Jack. (2006). *Hitchcock's Music*. Yale University Press.
Taylor-Johnson, Samantha (Director). (2015). *Fifty Shades of Grey* [Film] Focus Features, Michael De Luca Productions, Trigger Street Productions, Universal Pictures.
Whitehead, Deborah. (2013). When Religious 'Mommy Bloggers' Met 'Mommy Porn': Evangelical and Mormon Women's Responses to *Fifty Shades*. *Sexualities*, 16(8), pp. 915–931.
Williams, Linda. (1991). Film Bodies: Gender, Genre and Excess. *Film Quarterly*, 44(4), pp. 2–13.
Williams, Linda. (1993). Second Thoughts on Hard Core: American Obscenity and the Scapegoating of Deviance. In Gibson, Pamela Church, and Gibson, Roma (Eds). *Dirty Looks: Women, Pornography, Power* (pp. 38–63). BFI Publishing.

Williams, Linda. (1999). *Hard Core: Power, Pleasure and the 'Frenzy of the Visible.'* University of California Press.
Young, Alison. (1997). Murder in the Eyes of the Law. *Studies in Law, Politics, and Society*. 17, pp. 31–58.
Young, Miriam. (2016). *Singing the Body Electric: The Human Voice and Sound* Techn*ology*. Routledge.

Third Reading 2

Doing Jurisprudence with Your Body

The legal philosophy experienced sensationally by consumers of *the Scene* in *Fifty Shades of Grey* (Taylor-Johnson 2015) involves physical effort and agency. This is the kernel of this book's argument: consumers perform jurisprudence throughout their bodies while watching even the most maligned of cinema. This chapter details physical labours exerted by consumers enjoying and abhorring *the Scene* as they actively entertain alternative ways of understanding the legal ideas *shimmering* within it – evaluating possible trajectories of jurisprudential logic, weaving those into workable philosophical frameworks potentially applicable to a world beyond the cinema. This jurisprudence is about recognising legal concepts as sensations in the body, exercising their logics in conjunction with further legal ideas circulating through muscles, organs and blood, creating pleasurable or uncomfortable dissonance, juggling interpretations to reaffirm old ways of understanding law, altering them, feeling them differently and creating new ones – often sustaining multiple, conflicting theories of law simultaneously. Embodied legal theory at the cinema involves the activity and agency of corporeal thought, embodied decision-making and self-governance.

Mapping phenomenologically philosophical efforts exerted in the consumption of *the Scene*, I begin with the labours of cinematic agency in *loss of self* and *jouissance* – emphasising embodied decision-making, manipulation of format technologies, and self-stimulation. With reference to fan culture, I go on to show how consumers pursue gratifying dissonance and vacillation between suspending disbelief and active critical practice to deepen immersion and expand narrative worlds to achieve *affect* and experience further pleasure. The physicality of dissonance and vacillation involves bodily engagement, affective critique, and performative theorising – particularly of gender, race, and sexuality but also justice and law. Finally, I examine the way corporeal agency is integral to identification with characters and text. Multiple, embodied identification with characters and other elements of *the Scene* includes competing interpretations of law that resonate through viscera but also rely

DOI: 10.4324/9780429330414-10

on the agentic activity of those watching. Sound and arousal encourage and facilitate all of these efforts. Knowledge is felt and borne in the matter of consumer-bodies and thought is practised as consumers prepare and exert themselves, *as bodies*, to relish and loathe their chosen texts. They engage physiologically, labouring to increase both pleasure and discontent, experiencing ideas and generating meaning phenomenologically. When a cinematic moment like *the Scene* is reliant on legal concepts, those concepts are navigated with bodily exertion and through sensation, intensities of feeling and affect. Consumers evaluate legal ideas and theories through their flesh: they perform embodied jurisprudence.

Cinematic Agency

Bodily exertion is central to the enjoyment of screen-based texts, from film choice, through watching behaviour, interaction with format technology and pursuit of arousal. These are all examples of embodied agency as self-governance exerted to intensify cinematic pleasure. This is embodied cinematic agency. Consumers actively chase *loss of self* and *jouissance* at the movies. Consequently, as they suspend their disbelief and let go of their critical lens, consumers remain agentic. As bodies, they stay engaged. When enthusiastically throwing themselves into sensation, consumers are also negotiating the theories concerning law *shimmering* with availability through the affects of the text. Thus, I argue, *losing yourself* to *the Scene* is active phenomenological engagement with legal theory.

Cinematic agency begins prior to entering theatres in choosing and preparing for which film is viewed. Although consumers regularly compromise their film choice to prioritise collective viewing, agency is evident in negotiations and shared decision-making to plan cinemagoing (Srinivas 2002). In the West, choices are customarily made based on genre (Srinivas 2002). Anticipated bodily sensations associated with genre are key to these decisions (Williams 1991). Many avoid the dread of horror or tension of thrillers, the tears and heartache of drama, while others seek out the stirred outrage concerning injustice depicted in certain documentaries (Chaudhuri 2014). Romance is enjoyed for embodied undulations (tension and release) as each narrative overcomes hurdles towards the joy of climactic union. There can be tearful, humourous, even rageful gratification when feeling represented in some way by women's fiction. Meanwhile, pornography is often an intentional viewing choice with a range of anticipated bodily responses, not just sexual arousal but also humour, disgust, and discomfort (Paasonen 2007, 2010). Ideally, consumers enter theatres *willingly* offering themselves up to their text, hoping they will experience sensual immersion (Brophy 1984). Rather than falling back passively into the sensual embrace of a text, consumers seek out films offering triggers towards all kinds of affect.

More than seeking experience, consumers prepare and exert their bodies for maximum gratification. Srinivas (2002) juxtaposes Indian and Western cinemagoing cultures to disrupt assumptions about passive consumption. Rather than reading quiet Western viewing as inactive against Indian participatory and interactive viewing, Srinivas (160) argues both are embodied cultural practices, describing Western viewing as "highly disciplined activity." It involves the "joint action" of "quiet-attentive" watching through contained motor activity plus "heightened attention and concentration" exercised phenomenologically in "active silence" (Hanich 2010, 95). Physical dread during horror movies particularly illustrates the engaged embodiment of stillness (Hanich 2010). Consumers know what to expect and "lean forward," anticipating each generic trigger, searching for how it will arrive (187).

These ostensibly still bodies act. Preparing themselves, tense and aroused, horror consumers, for example, curl into their seats, cover their eyes, turn away, sit forward, squeeze companions' hands, clench their muscles, and release into the "overwhelm" of awe-full-ness (Hanich 2010, 193). Consumers physically create situations and ready their bodies for the best affective experience within a given cinematic opportunity (Lamerichs 2018, 209). These are embodied actions of preparedness and participation. *Loss of self* to the text is strengthened by active attention, material responses to signifying stimuli and embodied participation in genre convention. The reward from the play of tension and release resembles arousal to orgasm: *jouissance.*

Pornography consumption exemplifies the exertions of achieving *jouissance* with a screen text. Masturbation is just one method. Participatory agentic activity is also discernible in the fetishism of delivery format. Williams (1999) traces a history of pornography consumption from privately viewed late 19th century films, through mid-20th century public cinemas and peep shows, to late 20th century video cassettes and 21st century virtual reality equipment. Each technology contributes to the bodily delight of consumption or detracts due to discomfort, disgust, alienation, or other bodily conditions. The fetishization of each is about increased arousal through interaction with extratextual elements.

Arousal is further engorged through assertive exchanges with these technologies. Melendez (2004) demonstrates the erotic materiality of inserting a video cassette and working the remote control to pause, rewind, and rewatch. In this instance, the consumer merges with the text, their body mimicking those depicted on screen while enjoyment is enhanced by physical interaction with the delivery format, exerting control over the text. Even when pursuing *loss of self* in *jouissance* as orgasm, consumers are active and agentic, interacting with intertextual conditions, and exerting control over what they see and how technology delivers it to them.

Participatory enjoyment in *the Scene* begins with the choice to view *Fifty Shades* at the cinema – perhaps on Valentine's Day when its release day ticket sales broke various records (Gray 2015). Watching on release day can add to the excitement of cinema viewing, manifesting in greater discernible participation from audiences. Subsequently, during *the Scene*, consumers are encouraged to respond to the playful music and dramatic sounds with building enthusiasm and bodily tension. Indulging in the tantalising thrill of flirtation and tightening muscles – anticipating represented sex, consumer-bodies lean towards Christian's reading of Ana's alleged arousal. Such efforts are exploited by Ana's refusal while consumers are encouraged to simultaneously enjoy her triumph. Ultimately, consumers are rewarded for their labours through prolonged *jouissance*. Woven through their determination to get the most enjoyment from *the Scene* are legal ideas about how urgent it might feel to override non-consent and how arousing it might be negotiating and refusing a contract.

Concurrently, while consumers might quietly focus attention on the audio-visual scene, holding their bodies still, they may simultaneously notice their heightened sensory perception (they are aroused), attending to the texture of their clothes, seat fabric, arms almost touching neighbour's flesh, legs pressing against legs. They might become aware of the arousal of others in the cinema – perceiving the embodied jurisprudence of friends and strangers. Each layer of sensorial observation potentially deepens consumer pleasure. Noting and managing multiple points of sensation is agentic exercise.

But participatory enjoyment may not comply with the pornographic trajectory of *the Scene*. A consumer may release their tension early by sharing a derisive eye roll with companions or distort their breathing by sighing with frustration or groaning with feminist outrage. Sometimes consumers resist the inducements of conventional effects. Following, I demonstrate how embodied resistance to preferred sensational engagements with text can be deeply gratifying. Sometimes it is too hard to let go of cynicism or discomfort with the sensational logics of a text. Thus, although a consumer may have decided to attend a romance, prepared to feel aroused anticipation of union, they may not be willing or able to overcome disquiet with representations of violence as romance. This might be experienced as unease, dissatisfaction, or anger. Best efforts to be gratified by sensually stimulating signifiers might be thwarted by physiologically felt understandings of gender, sexuality, and law. In *the Scene* this could be recognition of exploitative control in the contract's terms, the violence of overwriting another's refusal to consent, or the scene's resemblance to workplace sexual harassment. Each of these resonates as violence. They are also legally meaningful, manifesting interpretations of law and legal concepts. Enjoying cinema depends upon embodied grappling with theoretically informed, physiologically stimulating content.

Immersive cinema consumption is not passive. Pleasurable *loss of self* is effectively and powerfully generated through active bodily participation. It involves agentic phenomenological activity, from negotiating film choice and preparing for genre triggers, to clenching and releasing muscles, and managing heightened sensorial perception for enhanced delight (or displeasure). Cinema enjoyment is not homogenous and may be contrary to that which is predicted or encouraged by its production. The effort discernible in consuming cinema for increased pleasure, together with the lack of homogeneity across active enjoyment, provides evidence towards recognising that consumers are considering numerous alternative phenomenological interpretations of film. These interpretive practices are agentic and include visceral grappling with legal theory and the creation of legal meaning.

Dissonance, Vacillation, and *Affective* Critique

Resistance to the affective triggers of screen-based texts can generate pleasures that consumers seek to indulge. Embodied active displeasure and affective critique are regularly practised in conjunction with effortful *loss of self* to reach *jouissance*. Vacillation between ostensibly contradictory perspectives provides further evidence of consumers exercising embodied philosophy – viscerally analysing and critiquing, rejecting, and accepting diverse ways of understanding. This is a return to the consumer agency established in *Reader Agency*. However, to demonstrate more clearly the corporeality of theoretical practice, I explore consumer dissonance and vacillation between immersive alignment with, and active criticism of, texts. Fan cultures exemplify such dissonance in both philosophical and physical ways, discernible in discussion forums, fan activism and cosplay. I argue that Feminist critics also pursue affective rewards and achieve phenomenological gratification by exercising their condemnation of *Fifty Shades* with their bodies, sharing their intensities of feeling by publishing their effortful interpretations. Correspondingly, enjoyment of *the Scene* can be enhanced by vacillating between uncritical merging with its diegetic world and criticism of the text. Implementing both modes of interpreting *the Scene* can deepen textual immersion and increase gratification and enjoyment. Threaded through these dissonant and vacillating interpretive practices are ideas about law, contract, and consent.

Feminist scholarship demonstrates that consumers of women's fiction exercise agency in their consuming practices, gaining pleasure by reading critically. The consumer agency mapped in *Reader Agency* includes simultaneously identifying with multiple characters, evaluating content, analysing representations of romance, and assessing narrative style and storytelling technique. Some of this critical work celebrates texts, some of it censures. Like Ang's (1985) *Dallas* viewers, a lot of consumers do both at once in a form of active dissonance or vacillation between indulgent enjoyment and condemnation. The dissonance of generating discordant interpretations of a text is often pleasurable and rewarding. Shifting between conflicting interpretations of a text can mean sometimes suspending disbelief, indulging in uncritical *loss of self*, and sometimes pursuing gratification through outrage, disappointment, cynicism, and mockery. When my friends and I watched *Twilight* we delighted in our shared complicated relationships with the film series, feeling outrage and desire, heteronormative joy, feminist shame, and a whole lot more, in quick succession. We also expressed self-deprecating reflective mockery – messaging each other with rapid typing on tiny phone screens, laughing out loud (lol) at ourselves and our guilty pleasures. Consumers of women's fiction pursue pleasure (*jouissance*?) through both merging with narrative worlds and being actively critical of them. Further than this, critique is a form of enriched immersion in text: devoting time to wrestling with the philosophical arguments available within. In this chapter, I am building on this knowledge about consumption to recognise that consumer agency is not only *felt* through the body but is *performed by bodies* as the exercise of embodied philosophy.

In *Fifty Shades* discussion forums, consumers generate gratifying sensations by vacillating between exuberant enjoyment and humorous and heated criticism. Jones and Mills (2014) and Deller and Smith (2013, 947) show forum participants gaining "considerable pleasure" from criticising *Fifty Shades*. Harman and Jones (2013, 952) suggest that most *Fifty Shades* consumers are "hate reading." Moreover, they propose that "undiscerning readers" do not exist "except as an imagined spectre" haunting feminist critics (961). Thus, rather than understanding *Fifty Shades* consumers as passive victims indoctrinated into accepting toxic heterosexuality, Harmon and Jones argue that consumers are reading *Fifty Shades* with critical awareness and pleasurable dissonance. There is an enjoyment in consuming *Fifty Shades* that derives from indulging "felt and embodied" responses to it that include critically judging its aesthetics and theoretical assumptions (Lamerichs 2018, 219).

Fan culture is similarly characterised by discordant interpretation. Dyer (2021) describes fandom as a "critical pedagogy" while Duggan (2022, 200) notes that immersion in texts coexists with attention to detail and "sharp, rigorous analysis." Authoring fanfiction, some fans rectify problems they see in original texts (Tosenberger 2008, 203). Slash fiction tells parallel narratives, switching characters' gender, race, and sexuality (Dyer 2021). Rewriting and transforming original texts involves identification and replication of key themes, narratives, and aesthetics – exercising critical analysis as well as creative authorship (Coppa 2017, 4). Fan authors then weave their own theories through those of the original text. Such philosophising labour is pronounced in the "political battlefield" of Harry Potter fandom (Duggan 2022, 148). The original series proselytises theories of "courage, duplicity, friendship, happiness, justice, love and ambition . . . good, evil, death and freedom" (Irwin and Bassham 2010, xi). Fan-authors knit their own theories into the ideologically shaped magical narrative Potter-verse, build new arguments and ways of understanding – often "correcting" the original to create more inclusive stories, adapting the logic of justice with greater complexities concerning sex, sexuality, gender, race, and friendship.

The vigour of fan theory became acutely apparent when original author, JK Rowling, published anti-trans opinions on social media. Many fans denounced her (Duggan 2022). However, not all abandoned Harry Potter. Instead, many asserted the primacy of *their* interpretations of gender, sexuality, and justice, continuing to integrate them into the philosophies and narratives they value from the Potter-verse (Duggan 2022, 148).

Fan labour is dextrous, theoretically-informed analytical work: extracting philosophical ideas from texts, relishing some, correcting or rejecting others, asserting new ways of understanding – even in opposition to the politics of original authors. In their dissonant and often vacillating relationship with their chosen original texts, these fans are *doing* theory.

Fan theory involves bodies. Critical engagement is corporeal as thought is embodied. However, further forms of corporeal labour are exercised in fan and consumer dissonance. This is especially discernible in cosplay. Fans labour to embody their interpretation of characters and other aspects of original texts. Creating costumes, cosplayers also rehearse movement and behaviour: they *become* their understanding of a text. They recreate the *grain* of their favourite characters with the whole of their bodies. All these efforts are undertaken to produce "optimal aesthetic experience[s]" felt throughout cosplayer bodies as affective pleasure (Lamerichs 2018, 209). Cosplayers labour philosophically as fan-authors do, to identify and replicate a text's aesthetics so their costume is recognisable; they prepare their bodies both in terms of costume and performance and in anticipation of bodily enjoyment – *jouissance* – sharing performative merging with texts (209). Linking the politics of slash fiction and the corporeal interpretation of cosplay I propose that analytical consumer labour includes performative theorising of sex, sexuality, gender, race, class, justice, law, and further philosophies available in the interaction between text and consumer. Immersive *jouissance* through cosplay entails embodied dissonance and vacillation between *losing the self* to a text's philosophically rich universe and critical navigations of its arguments and assumptions through performances of theory as embodiments of each consumer's interpretation.

Buying sex toys and exploring new ways of doing sex inspired by *Fifty Shades* is similar to cosplay. "[A]ffectivity is crucial" to cosplayers (Lamerichs 2018, 218). It is also central to *Fifty Shades* consumers exploring their sexuality. Both seek to extend the sensual experiences of a text, feeling the *grain* of characters and storylines to *lose the self* in narrative universes and reach *jouissance*. All of this involves performative experimenting with theories of sex, sexuality, and gender. Buying sex toys inspired by *Fifty Shades* is embodied theoretical practice through cinema consumption, with consumers seeking to recreate the *grain* – the imagined textures and intensities of feeling – of the film's pornographic aesthetic, exploring alternative ways of imagining and doing sex, sexuality, and gender.

Whitehead's (2013) analysis of conservative religious women's blogs provides evidence that *Fifty Shades* inspired imagining of and doing sex differently involves theory. Her study observes Mormon and Evangelical Christian women bloggers philosophically juxtaposing logic accessible in *Fifty Shades* with their own theological understandings and lived experiences of sex, sexuality, and gender. Some of the bloggers condemn *Fifty Shades*, arguing that, for example, BDSM runs counter to their religious values. Others welcome the books as an opportunity to address issues of gendered violence. Further bloggers celebrate *Fifty Shades* as enabling recognition of women's desire within the sanctity of marriage and thereby supporting their Christian principles. One blog recounts conservative religious women using the books to talk "openly and honestly" about their experiences of sex and relationships. Each of these women weaves their phenomenological knowledges with the texts, feeling their pornographic and romantic affects, reflecting on their intimate relationships with husbands and with Christ (quite specifically) and their own desire – contemplating and doing sex differently.

The embodied quality of this theory work is not only about doing sex but also includes the physicality of writing blogs, participating in online discussion forums, writing feminist criticism, and collaborating with fellow fans to produce fiction and art. These activities are performed by reading eyes, typing fingers, reacting organs, and nerve endings, endorphin and hormone-producing glands, and muscles working whole bodies to cut, sew, glue, paint, dress, and perform cosplay, music, and videos. Fans exert themselves when providing critical feedback to each other in loops of "gift exchange," enriching and refining their products (Jones 2014). The remuneration of the exchange is not monetary but intellectual and affective, dealing in intensities of feeling (Jones 2014; Coppa 2017). Kelley (2021) calls it an "emotion economy." Meanwhile, emerging evidence in friendship-focused neuroscience shows that interactions and anticipation of interactions with friends, imagining simultaneously experiencing emotions, and consuming cultural products together all trigger reward-related activity in the brain and influence the brain's biological structure (Güroğlu 2022). This science potentially measures the affective delights of sharing critical evaluations of text, experiencing others' analytical appreciation of one's work, recognising one's ideas materialised in the work of another, and crafting creative objects (like fanfiction, art, costumes) together. Collaborative interactions and fan-based friendships are experienced phenomenologically as embodied intensities of feeling and sensation – altering the biological structure of brains. Integral to these friendships are dissonant and vacillating critical, analytical immersive engagements with text.

I propose that although feminist critics articulate genuine concern and awareness of gendered violence in the world and *Fifty Shades*, their expressions of fear and outrage can be read within the same range of dissonant and vacillating sensational immersive engagement and productive critical enjoyment of text as that present in fan culture. Critics gain gratification through their critical engagement with texts and their production of secondary texts, all the while experiencing and performing theory – *losing themselves* to intensities of feeling: discomfort, outrage, disgust, and fear. Their affective responses are informed by their feminist philosophy – their possible awareness of gender as a social construct that shapes violence in intimate relationships, and their knowledge and understanding of how law does and should work to support or prevent such violence. When the feminist critics write their blogs, scholarly articles and news pieces, they are extending their philosophically-informed phenomenological experience of *Fifty Shades* – their derisive amusement, anger, and fear – and expanding the story universe beyond the original text in ways similar to fans. They mix their bodies with the theories of sex, gender, sexuality, and law *shimmering* within *Fifty Shades*. They also generate meaning through their *affective* responses to the text's offered conceptualisations of legal tools.

Additionally, I propose that feminist critics enjoy similar phenomenological rewards as fan-authors, thereby further exercising theory through their bodies. For instance, their labour to transform dissonant *loss of self* in, and critical analysis of, *Fifty Shades* into secondary texts (news media pieces; academic articles) stimulates gratification. Such intensity of feeling is strengthened by the emotion economy and gift exchange provided through comment sections and collegial feedback. Like fans, feminist critics imagine sharing consumption of cultural texts, and sharing emotional reactions to them; they anticipate and experience interactions with like-minded friends and readers through the publication, consumption, and reactions to their critiques. In these ways, brain-altering neurological rewards are stimulated by their interpretative, analytical and philosophical work. From the acts of reading and writing to the pleasures of imagining sharing intensities of feeling, philosophy is exercised, and affects are generated throughout the bodies of feminist critics.

Harman and Jones (2013) speculate that most readers are hate-reading *Fifty Shades* in similar ways as the feminist critics. Jones and Mills (2014) and Bonomi et al. (2016) evidence comparable dissonant or vacillating consumer enjoyment. I suggest that such shared critical engagement echoes the theoretically informed fan work and embodied enjoyment, including the possible stimulated changes in brain biology.

Pursuing the *affects* of dissonance while consuming cinema involves simultaneously entertaining alternative interpretations of text in the matter of the body. Vacillation requires agentic shifting between corporeal engagement with conventional affective triggers to achieve *loss of self*, and embodied critical analysis, resisting those triggers, and indulging intensities of feeling derision, discomfort, fear, and rage. These phenomenological interactions with text hold in them ideas and ideologies. Dissonance and vacillation navigate numerous diverging interpretations, multivarious lines of logic and manifold philosophies. Like cosplay, buying sex toys inspired by *Fifty Shades* exemplifies the corporeality of dissonance and vacillation, evidencing the embodied performance of consumer theorising. Further, *Fifty Shades* consumers talking about their relationships and sex lives, buying sex toys, and experimenting with different ways of doing sex is performing their understandings of sex, gender, sexuality, and law with their typing fingers, clenching muscles, and reacting organs. As they type, make purchases, and do sex they are also physically exploring different theories and creating new meanings about what it is to be gendered, what (non)consensual sex feels like, how ethical sex can work, what sensations of intimacy mean. Such corporeal theorising is practised more inconspicuously when each consumer sits in the cinema. Because legal knowledge is also born by bodies and saturates screen-based texts, consumers are actively grappling with theories of law with their bodies as they watch even the most maligned of fiction at the cinema.

Agentic Embodied Identification

My final example of corporeal cinematic jurisprudence involves *agentic* embodied identification. Like *losing oneself* in a text, embodied identification requires consumer effort as well as evaluative exploration of different ways of understanding. While sound and arousal facilitate identification through the matter of bodies, the sense of feeling with a character or other components of a text relies on the work of a consumer to *do* the identifying. Consumers labour to feel empathically connected and enhance their enjoyment of a text by exploring multiple lines of identification, simultaneously processing content from the perspectives of various characters. In *the Scene*, the exercise of manifold embodied empathy includes exploring, evaluating and reconceptualising legal ideas as sensation and intensities of feeling. Attending to the agency of embodied identification makes visible the way that consumer efforts at multiple simultaneous identification can enhance enjoyment towards *jouissance*. It also helps to detect the physical labour of theorising sex, gender, sexuality, and law performed by consumers watching *the Scene*. The sensational wrangling with multiple opportunities for embodied identification is jurisprudence practised by consumer-bodies watching *Fifty Shades*.

In the previous chapter, I demonstrated how sound and arousal facilitate consumers' identification with cinematic characters and ideas by stirring intensities of feeling throughout their bodies. Folk sitting in cinemas watching *the Scene* are prompted to experience affects that align with characters and aspects of the text as though they are part of the action. Because *the Scene* is all about negotiating a contract, consent, intimacy, and sex, consumers are encouraged to feel multiple interpretations of law as they identify with Christian's pressing desire, Ana's triumphant refusal, the corporate *mis-en-scène*, the flirty-to-tense music, and the narrative drive through arousing undulations towards possible climax. Conspiracies of sound, plot, dialogue, shot sequencing, and so much more, urge consumer-bodies to deeply, empathically identify with theories of law available in the text. I argue that this embodied identification is agentic: consumers exert control, make decisions, and self-govern even as they respond to affective triggers, seemingly without awareness, with their beating hearts, heightened perceptions, leaking tear ducts, and clenching muscles.

The pleasure and labour of embodied identification are regularly about playing with multiple lines of empathic connection simultaneously. Doty's (1993, xiv) "moments of 'multiple queerness'" speak of the abundance of possible points of identification coexisting. Although they co-occur, they are distinct from each other and "sometimes contradictory" (xiv). This echoes Steinbock's (2019) trans* *shimmers* through which opportunities for identification are endless, though often potentially fleeting, and dependent upon the angle of each consumer's arrival. Queer reading accommodates concurrent exploration of manifold perspectives and experiences. This is because, according to Doty (1993, xvi), queer reading is more than interpreting a text's offerings as they align with one identity but "can also be about the intersecting or combining of more than one specific form of nonstraight sexuality." More particularly, it might "accumulate lesbian, gay and bisexual [trans*, nonbinary, asexual . . .] responses, sometimes in relation to the same spectator" (Doty 1993, xvi). Cross-identification, as Steinbock (2019) writes, is "less uncommon" than often theorised in cinema studies and is potentially available to everyone.

Girl readers engage with their fiction by shifting perspective and identifying with more than one character at a time, as well as other aspects of their texts. In demonstrating girl readers' agentic agility, Kapurch (2016, 18) stresses the work they do to "imagine other characters' points of view." Blackford (2004, 19) shows these girls actively shifting perspective while they read. Meanwhile, Duggan (2022, 152) describes queer reading as a continual *act* of "paying attention to the subtextual or surface level queer elements of texts." The pervasiveness of queerness in texts *shimmers* to be glimpsed, grasped, *felt* – enjoyed as empathic connection or identification with the perspective of another person, character, and textual viewpoint. Scholarship documenting these consumers demonstrates the agency and effort exerted by consumers as they enjoy the embodied perspectives of more than one character or aspect of a text at a time.

Pendleton (1992) is emphatic that the relationship between text and consumer is dialectic. More specifically, he determines that screen-based text, and pornography in particular, "does not program people" (156). He argues that gay pornography provided a rare opportunity for men to explore non-heteronormative sexualities and masculinities when, in the late twentieth century, representations of gay men were limited and much maligned. He counters concerns about cinema (pornography, horror, action) indoctrinating viewers into ostensibly deviant behaviours (see Boyle 2000, 2005; Young 2009). Rather than being "programmed," he argues that gay men "play with pornography." He talks about *finding* your "kink" – *discovering* what style of sex delights you, which acts excite, which partners, locations, and toys thrill. As "play" this is far from passive, but active exploration and engagement with effort, (possibly including the manual labour of masturbation). While porn enables the trying on of "different positions, fantasies, kinks," the consumer must *do* the work of *trying on* (Pendleton 1992, 155–156). Pornography is a tool consumers can use to experiment with lines of identification that are very much about sensation, affect, and intensities of feeling. Using porn, consumers *visit* "distant realms" (Paasonen 2018); *experiment* with various "versions of self-in-society" (Barker in Paasonen 2018, 544); *play* imaginatively with previously untried ways of doing sex, of being and of understanding (Williams 1999). I use italics to draw attention to verbs describing the activity, labour, and effort exerted by consumers in their identification with text.

Like the arousal of pornography, music's apparent capacity to cause consumers to physiologically identify with texts masks labour and agency. While we can understand music to open consumers up to the experiences and perspectives of another person who is significantly different from themselves (Young 2016), this identification relies on efforts exerted by each consumer. Kheshti's (2008) critique of listener identification reveals the agency and activity of consumers in these experiences. She analyses "World Music" consumption, through which Globally Northern listeners feel empathic connection with musicians from the Global South. Using an exemplifying piece, "S'Ma" (*Arabian Journeys* Kinship Records 2001) Kheshti notes the absent crediting of the vocalist providing the piece's most striking affective *grain*. The words they sing are not in the language of the target audience. The listener feels enriched through a deep empathy they experience when hearing the voice of someone dramatically culturally different from themselves, someone from another culture. But this voice also appears to be part of other uncredited sounds from the same unidentified exotic location. Kheshti emphasises that the connection to the voice is *imagined* by the listener. The richness of the identification and the meaning generated by the listener's empathy relies on the embodied imaginative labour of the listener.

Kheshti's (2008) Globally Northern listener imagines and *feels* that they are opening themselves up to and gaining insight into the life of someone radically different from themselves. However, the accuracy of their imagination is reliant on their pre-existing knowledge and their self-education about the lived experiences of those with whom they "identify." The vocalist is not present to interact with the listener, to challenge suppositions or to add complexity and dimension to the representation. And yet, because their vocalisation is experienced through the consumer's body (and imagined as made through the body of the vocalist), it can feel very real and very connected for the listener. The listener *feels* they *are* empathising throughout their bodies with the imagined body of the vocalist.

Kheshti (2015) argues that this embodied sense of identification bolsters colonial relations by obscuring the subjectivity of the vocalist, exoticising them as a nameless other – part of the generalised sound environment of an unknown culture. The vocalist does not articulate words discernible to the Northern consumer; the vocalist is not presented with agency or authorship; they do not exert influence over the text or its consumption. Meanwhile, the listener retains agency and subjecthood: controlling the format technology through which they hear the music (play, pause, volume), and through their exertion of imaginative labour – imagining the material form of the *grain of the voice* perhaps even replicating the sound of the vocalist without knowing the words they are attempting to reproduce. Viscerally experienced identification with sound involves the exertion of consumers' ability to act and the action of consumers to both produce feelings of deep identification and to make meaning from that sense of connection. The labour of identification is rewarding for the Globally Northern listener because the experienced depth of their identification to a Globally Southern person enhances their self-worth and "virtue signals" to increase their social capital. In Kheshti's analysis, sonically facilitated agentic embodied identification with World Music is shaped by colonial ideology and is gratifying when exercised along colonial lines, thus reinforcing the apparent validity of colonial logic. The listener's exercise of agentic embodied identification works colonial ideology through their flesh.

Agentic embodied identification with *the Scene* similarly works ideology (theoretical understandings) through consumer-bodies. However, because the structure of *the Scene* encourages multiple simultaneous opportunities for identification, the ideologies are also manifold. This means that the consumer is juggling or negotiating dissonant ways of understanding. I argue that negotiating different ways of understanding is theoretical practice.

Pleasure in consuming *the Scene* is potentially enhanced by agentic simultaneous embodied identification with both characters and other elements of the text. This includes preparing for anticipated body genre triggers to best achieve *loss of self* and working the body to enjoy arousal in physical empathy with Christian's desire to "fuck" Ana. We are encouraged to pursue some measure of sexual climax as resolution. Such physical investment makes Ana's refusal to consent to sex and contract potentially frustrating. It might feel particularly abrupt if we have also enjoyed Ana's sensually extended arm and question about whether the sex would happen on the table. We may have used her actions to intensify our sensations in line with her ostensible arousal.

However, by concurrently entertaining Ana's perspective, we can also feel her triumphantly asserted bodily autonomy, leaving *the Scene* without signing or having sex. Simultaneous multiple identification combines vexed desire with triumphant refusal to create an undulating minor climax within a prolonged gratifying consumption of a women's fiction that might be akin to *feminine jouissance*.

Woven through this physical labour are various theories of law. Enjoying the thrill of Ana's refusal involves investment in a liberal feminist interpretation of contract as empowering Ana with control over her bodily autonomy and protecting her from gendered violence. At the same time, pursuing arousal through active embodied identification with Christian involves entertaining masculinist understandings of "reasonably" discerning consent on the surfaces of a woman's body (even when it contradicts the woman's words), that consent is nonretractable, and climax retroactively provides consent. Identifying with and feeling the *shimmers* of Ana's uncertainty can strengthen pessimistic poststructural feminist theories that contract and consent paradoxically promise equality and bodily autonomy while failing to empower, and ultimately blaming survivors for the violence against them. These embodied lines of understanding how law works, how negotiating a contract feels, and what consent looks and feels like are tangled up with consumers' participatory entertainment of characters' perspectives.

Sound and arousal facilitate explorations of another's perspective, ways of understanding, which are felt as intensities of feeling. Such exploration relies on the pre-existing knowledge, philosophical range, and labour of each consumer. Thus, although the text may support cross-identification enabling consumers to feel with characters radically different from themselves, each consumer must do the imaginative "trying-on," experimenting, and playing. More than this, Kheshti demonstrates the *control* consumers exercise over embodied identification. While the empathy a consumer feels with an element of a text, the quality of that empathy relies on the willingness of the consumer to lose themselves, plus their pre-existing knowledge and analytical skill. It is reliant on their "angle of arrival." In *the Scene*, consumers are encouraged to play with the perspectives of two characters through the matter of their bodies: to feel desire and triumphant refusal. Further theoretically informed intensities of feeling are available to consumers. Part of the enjoyment of watching is derived from entertaining conflicting intensities of feeling. Each perspective concerns the contract that is under negotiation and the consent that is being withheld and potentially overwritten. Both legal tools, in the context of sex, are laden with assumptions about sex, gender, sexuality, and law – including ideas about law's authority and capacity to empower, support ethical negotiations over intimacy or gaslight the marginalised. Felt in bodies as part of multiple simultaneous embodied identifications, this is corporeal theorising of law.

Theorising Law with Your Body at the Cinema

In this chapter, I have detailed corporeal efforts exercised by consumers enjoying and abhorring texts with agency, self-governance, and embodied decision-making. This ranges from choosing and preparing for film-viewing with consideration of body genres, manipulating technology, and working muscle and sensory organs and tissue for maximum gratification. It ranges through the exercise of those sensory engagements as *loss of self* to a text, and simultaneous or vacillating critique. This includes pursuing *frisson* through dissonant love-hating a text. And it ranges to consumers actively "trying on" and "playing with" various, often multiple, potential lines of identification available in each scene, imaginatively experiencing the movement, emotional reactions, and intensities of feeling of screen bodies, through their own bodies. Immersive cinema consumption is generated through active agentic bodily participation.

Woven through consumers' active corporeal efforts to obtain gratification and *jouissance* are manifold theories about so many things like sex, gender, and sexuality. Theories of law are also present. The agentic effort exerted to enjoy and *lose oneself* in a text provides evidence towards recognising consumers considering various possible phenomenological interpretations of a film. Pursuing the *affects* of dissonance or vacillation between *loss of self* and critical analysis involves willing enjoyment of conventionally presented ways of understanding such things as sex, gender, sexuality, and law. It involves exploring and asserting theories that *shimmer* more fleetingly within texts, accessible along the angles of each consumer's arrival. It also involves the delights of reading against or countering dominant theories available in a text. Theory is also performed in embodied identification because part of the "trying on" of possibly multiple perspectives is entertainment of different ways of comprehending the content of a scene. In *the Scene*, the multiple perspectives are differing interpretations of how the specific legal tools of contract and consent work in the context of heterosexual intimacy. The agency with which consumers navigate theoretically informed *affects* determines that they are doing more than feeling legal ideas and theories – they are practising theory with their bodies. The combination of agency and legal ideas exercised through bodies with sensation and intensities of feeling is the performance of jurisprudence. People theorise law with their bodies while watching *the Scene* from *Fifty Shades of Grey*.

Bibliography

Ang, Ien. (1985). *Watching Dallas: Soap Opera and the Melodramatic Imagination*. Taylor and Franci.

Blackford, Holly Virginia. (2004). *Out of This World: Why Literature Matters to Girls*. Teachers College Press.

Bonomi, Amy E., Nichols, Emily M., Carotta, Christin L., Kiuchi, Yuya, and Perry, Samantha. (2016). Young Women's Perceptions of the Relationship in Fifty Shades of Grey. *Journal of Women's Health*, 25(2), pp. 139–148.

Boyle, Karen. (2000). The Pornography Debates: Beyond Cause and Effect. *Women's Studies International Forum*, 23(2), pp. 187–195.

Boyle, Karen. (2005). *Media and Violence: Gendering the Debates*. Sage Publications.

Brophy, Philip. (1984). Tales of Terror. *Cinema Papers*, 49, pp. 400–407.

Chaudhuri, Shohini. (2014). *Cinema of the Dark Side: Atrocity and the Ethics of Film Spectatorship*. Edinburgh University Press.

Coppa, Francesca. (2017). *The Fanfiction Reader: Folk Tales for the Digital Age*. University of Michigan Press.

Deller, Ruth A., and Smith, Clarissa. (2013). Reading the BDSM Romance: Reader Responses to Fifty Shades. *Sexualities*, 16(8), pp. 932–950.

Doty, Alexander. (1993). Whose Text is It Anyway?: Queer Cultures, Queer Auteurs, and Queer Authorship. *Quarterly Review of Film & Video*, 15(1), pp. 41–54.

Duggan, Jennifer. (2022). Transformative Readings: Harry Potter Fan Fiction, Trans/Queer Reader Response, and J. K. Rowling. *Children's Literature in Education*, 53, pp. 147–168.

Dyer, Connor. (2021). Critical Pedagogy and Visual Culture Art Education in a Cosplay-Based Curriculum. *Transformative Works and Cultures*, 35, no pagination.

Gray, Brandon. (February 16, 2015). Weekend Report: Valentine's Day Massacres Presidents' Day Record. *Box Office Mojo*. www.boxofficemojo.com/article/ed2658796548/

Güroğlu, Berna. (2022). The Power of Friendship: The Developmental Significance of Friendships from a Neuroscience Perspective. *Child Development Perspectives*, 16(2), pp. 110–117.

Hanich, Julian. (2010). *Cinematic Emotion in Horror Films and Thrillers the Aesthetic Paradox of Pleasurable Fear*. Routledge.

Harman, Sarah, and Jones, Bethan. (2013). Fifty Shades of Ghey: Snark Fandom and the Figure of the Anti-Fan. *Sexualities*, 16(8), pp. 951–968.

Irwin, William, and Bassham, Gregory. (2010). Introduction: Harry Potter and the Enchantment of Philosophy. In Irwin, William, and Bassham, Gregory (Eds). *The Ultimate Harry Potter and Philosophy: Hogwarts for Muggles* (pp. 1–7). John Wiley & Sons.

Jones, Bethan. (2014). Fifty Shades of Exploitation: Fan Labor and Fifty Shades of Grey. *Transformative Works and Cultures*, 15, pp. 115–123.

Jones, Lucy, and Mills, Sara. (2014). Analysing Agency: Reader Responses to Fifty Shades of Grey. *Gender and Language*, 8(2), pp. 225–244.

Kapurch, Katie. (2016). *Victorian Melodrama in the Twenty-First Century*. Palgrave.

Kelley, Brit. (2021). *Loving Fanfiction: Exploring the Role of Emotion in Online Fandoms*. Routledge.

Kheshti, Roshanak. (2008). Inversion, Significance and the Loss of the Self in Sound. *Parallax*, 14(2), pp. 68–77.

Kheshti, Roshanak. (2015). *Modernity's Ear: Listening to Race and Gender in World Music*. New York University Press.
Kinship Records (Producer). (2001). *S'Ma Arabian Journeys* [Audio Recording].
Lamerichs, Nicolle. (2018). *Productive Fandom*. Amsterdam University Press.
Melendez, Franklin. (2004). Video Pornography, Visual Pleasure. In Williams, Linda (Ed). *Porn Studies* (pp. 401–428). Duke University Press.
Paasonen, Susanna. (2007). Strange Bedfellows: Pornography, Affect and Feminist Reading. *Feminist Theory*, 8(1), pp. 43–57.
Paasonen, Susanna. (2010). Disturbing, Fleshy Texts: Close Looking at Pornography. In Paasonen, Susanna, and Liljeström, Marianne (Eds). *Working with Affect in Feminist Readings: Disturbing Differences* (pp. 58–71). Taylor and Francis
Paasonen, Susanna. (2018). Many Splendored Things: Sexuality, Playfulness and Play. *Sexualities*, 21(4), pp. 537–551.
Pendleton, David. (1992). Obscene Allegories: Narrative, Representation, Pornography. *Discourse*, 15(1), pp. 154–168.
Srinivas, Lakshmi. (2002). The Active Audience: Spectatorship, Social Relations and the Experience of Cinema in India. *Media, Culture & Society*, 24(2), pp. 155–173.
Steinbock, Eliza. (2019). *Shimmering Images: Trans Cinema, Embodiment, and the Aesthetics of Change*. Duke University Press.
Taylor-Johnson, Samantha (Director). (2015). *Fifty Shades of Grey* [Film] Focus Features, Michael De Luca Productions, Trigger Street Productions, Universal Pictures.
Tosenberger, Catherine. (2008). Homosexuality at the Online Hogwarts: Harry Potter Slash Fanfiction. *Children's Literature*, 36(1), pp. 185–207.
Whitehead, Deborah. (2013). When Religious 'Mommy Bloggers' Met 'Mommy Porn': Evangelical and Mormon Women's Responses to Fifty Shades. *Sexualities*, 16(8), pp. 915–931.
Williams, Linda. (1991). Film Bodies: Gender, Genre and Excess. *Film Quarterly*, 44(4), pp. 2–13.
Williams, Linda. (1999). *Hard Core: Power, Pleasure and the 'Frenzy of the Visible'*. University of California Press.
Young, Alison. (2009). *The Scene of Violence: Cinema, Crime, Affect*. Routledge.
Young, Miriam. (2016). *Singing the Body Electric: The Human Voice and Sound Technology*. Routledge.

Postlude – Embodied Legal Philosophy Beyond the Cinema and Jurisprudential Sex

Jurisprudence is knowledge, philosophy and theory pertaining to what law is, how it works and what it ought to be. To "theorise" is to formulate or contemplate abstractly, (speculatively, hypothetically) a conceptualisation or understanding of something. Theory, and particularly legal theory, is usually treated within academia as reliant on general principles established through dedicated scholarship and only known through formal education. However, I propose that abstract, hypothetical, and speculative conceptualisations of law are practised by each person every day with their bodies. It is ordinary and productive. Continual embodied legal philosophy materialises law makes legal ideas meaningful – gives them form and life. Each person's theorising of law manifests in their bodies as sensation, intensities of feeling, states of being, identities, choices, actions, and behaviour. Legal interpretation becomes flesh as it is felt, smelt, tasted, thought, and performed by bodies, and bodies *become* a bit legal along the trajectories of each interpretation. Our molecules mingle with potentially multiple divergent legal interpretations, however momentarily. As consumers, when we fold affectively or sensationally born legal ideas through the matter of our being, our understanding of the world, ourselves, and law morph, and law *becomes* a little different too. Law's meaning and reality are shaped by our everyday, incidental corporeal interpretations. Embodied popular jurisprudence makes law as much as legislation, precedent, and academic scholarship.

To argue for an understanding of embodied jurisprudence, I have demonstrated that multiple interpretations of law are available within a less than three-minute scene from a much-maligned but high-grossing erotic (pornographic) romance film, *the Scene* in *Fifty Shades of Grey* (Taylor-Johnson 2015). These interpretations are felt by consumer-bodies in cinemas as limbs haunted by memories and fantasies of movement, organs reverberating with sound, muscles clenching in anticipation, nerves excited by music, and genitals aroused by representational promises of sex. Consumers of genres best known for provoking *affect* grapple with the corporeal cinematic legal interpretations *shimmeringly* available in their texts. Body genre devotees labour

DOI: 10.4324/9780429330414-11

to immerse themselves in the logics of their chosen film's narrative universe, *losing themselves* to the pleasures of conventional effects and affects, feeling cinematically philosophical offerings, trying on various political arguments, playing with theories of sex, gender, sexuality . . . *and law*. These consumers also gain significant corporeal pleasure by exerting embodied critique, analysing texts at multiple levels, attending to shimmering nuances accessible through the angle of their arrival with their uniquely "acculturated sensorium" (Sobchack 1992), trained and *experienced* bodies (Ott 2010). Humour, unease, and condemnation are shared between some consumers, while others "correct" their texts by weaving their own theories into those of the original. Throughout this book, I have argued that counter to concerns articulated by *Fifty Shades'* feminist critics, *Fifty Shades* consumers use their bodies to engage with texts critically, dextrously, and with agency. Integral to their embodied critical engagement is law.

More specifically, theorising law is fundamental to the corporeal pleasure of consuming *the Scene* in *Fifty Shades*. The clash between Ana and Christian's separate understandings and use of contract and consent encourages consumers to pursue *jouissance* by generating gratifyingly dissonant embodied legal arguments. Cinematic effects incite arousal, urging consumers to ignore their possible disquiet about the contract's controlling terms – its resemblance to patriarchal oppression of women through marriage, recent legal formulations of intimate partner violence, and consent-defined sexual offences. The urgency of arousal incites consumer complicity with Christian overwriting Ana's non-consent to sex, reading desire – and thus consent – in her body. However, these consumers are simultaneously emboldened to enjoy Ana's triumphant, contractually empowered resistance as they hear the sound of stiletto heels when she exits the boardroom – leaving Christian, the proposed sex, and the unsigned contract. Unfulfilled desire to see sex in *the Scene* becomes an undulation of delayed gratification within the prolonged feminine *jouissance* of this example of women's fiction. Part of the enjoyment of this pornographically romantic moment – part of its arousal – is the adversarial consideration of multiple theories of how contract and consent work in the context of heterosexual sex and intimacy. Performing legal theory through the body is core to the pleasure of *the Scene*.

Corporeal jurisprudence is written into cinematic material to be practised by consumer-bodies for enhanced pleasure. Consumers implicitly entertain multiple interpretations of law even while *losing themselves* to *affective* textures – feeling the *grain* of *the Scene's* representations of law – in pursuit of *jouissance*. Corporeal jurisprudence is performed by consumers who concerned feminists imagine are passively vulnerable to what they consume. Consumers are interpreting law and shaping legal meaning.

Throughout Embodiment and Legal Theory, my focus has been on cinema as a site of jurisprudence, and particularly of jurisprudence performed by bodies with no specific legal training. Bodies are ostensibly "at leisure" or rest in front of films, passively, and uncritically absorbing ideas about romance, violence, gender, sexuality, and sex in dream-like states. And yet, cinema is experienced through sensations and intensities of feeling and is enjoyed through bodily preparation, with concerted effort, quiet attention, and active focus, processing sensation, and exercising muscles and organs for greatest affect. The meaning of cinema is dependent upon the interpretative physiological labour of those watching. The corporeal quality of theory is particularly discernible in cinema, making cinema a useful location for exploring embodied legal theory.

However, I propose in this conclusion that cinematic embodied legal theory is part of a broader phenomenon of corporeal jurisprudence. As physical beings, we continually theorise law with the whole of our bodies as its terms restrict, enable, and compel our movements, expressions, and sensations. As we move through our social world obeying and disobeying regulation, enjoying rights or living with the physical reality of our rights denied; when we resist law's directives, ignore and criticise legislation, we give law meaning, making material our lawfully shaped intensities of feeling and affects. We theorise law with the whole of our bodies all of the time. We perform embodied jurisprudence.

Building on the example of *Fifty Shades*, with evidence suggesting that consumers have been inspired to reflect on their intimate relationships, the role of sex in their theology, buying sex toys, and trying different ways of doing sex, I suggest that even in our most ostensibly intimate and desire-driven activities we are performing jurisprudence. We are performing jurisprudential sex.

Pornography research explores ways in which consumers use porn to "try on" or "play with" different kinks, gender, sexualities, and bodily practices (Pendleton 1992; Paasonen 2018; Williams 1999). The capacity of pornography to facilitate such experimentation is about the embodied interaction between the screen and consumer body. Vacillation between ostensibly passive letting go into, and active physical pursuit of, "loss of self," embodied empathic identification with elements of a text, and critique of a text. Consumers use cinematic effects and techniques for affecting arousal to imagine with the whole of their bodies what it feels like to do sex in the ways offered by their texts. These experiments might be taken out of the screen-consuming context to be pursued more extensively alone or with others. The phenomenologically imagined "trying on" thus becomes performative play or praxis. Correspondingly, when *Fifty Shades* consumers blog or chat with friends and strangers about sex and relationships, when they buy sex toys and experiment with "kinky fuckery," they are performatively extending their embodied experimentation beyond the quiet attention of the cinema and into their daily lives.

With the sex in *Fifty Shades* so tightly woven with its central narrative concerning contract and consent, the exploratory performances of sex inspired by *Fifty Shades* are textured by legal interpretation. Introducing sex toys and kink into sexual play is potentially informed by embodied identification with Ana's triumph within *the Scene* which is a realisation of liberal legal feminist theory that contract and consent can empower women to better exercise autonomy and sexual integrity within heterosexual intimacy. The vortex of embodied jurisprudence and consuming *Fifty Shades* may heighten the pleasure of performing the Submissive with a Dominant sexual partner who orchestrates sex – either by determining the terms of intimacy in a contractual manner (proposing activities and gaining consent), or assuming implied or ongoing consent and requiring obedience. Both of these imaginary scenarios describe intensities of feeling during intimacy that are shaped by embodied jurisprudence exercised during the consumption of *Fifty Shades of Grey*.

My purpose here reaches beyond arguing that consuming *Fifty Shades* influences consumers' experiences of sex. I am seeking to theorise that sex, within and beyond the context of consuming *Fifty Shades*, is jurisprudence. Within each sexual encounter we exercise legal theory with our bodies – this includes nonverbal communication of consent, the complex and inconsistent, even dissonant intensities of feeling about what consensual and nonconsensual sex feels like, as well as all the other negotiations over how we might give and receive pleasure and achieve phallic orgasm or prolonged feminine *jouissance*. Interpretations of law are felt and exercised throughout our flesh all the time. And while legislators, lawyers and academics create law in black letters, we make it material as we live out our interpretations of what it means, its authority over us and how it should be, even when we are having sex.

Bibliography

Ott, Brian. (2010). The Visceral Politics of *V for Vendetta*: On Political Affect in Cinema. *Critical Studies in Media Communication*, 27(1), pp. 39–54.

Paasonen, Susanna. (2018). Many Splendored Things: Sexuality, Playfulness and Play. *Sexualities*, 21(4), pp. 537–551.

Pendleton, David. (1992). Obscene Allegories: Narrative, Representation, Pornography. *Discourse*, 15(1), pp. 154–168.

Sobchack, Vivian Carol. (1992). *The Address of the Eye: A Phenomenology of Film Experience*. Princeton University Press.

Taylor-Johnson, Samantha (Director). (2015). *Fifty Shades of Grey* [Film] Focus Features, Michael De Luca Productions, Trigger Street Productions, Universal Pictures.

Williams, Linda. (1999). *Hard Core: Power, Pleasure and the 'Frenzy of the Visible'*. University of California Press.

Index